1992 – The Struggle for Europe

Also available from Berg by the same authors:

The Breakdown of Austin Rover: A Case-Study in the Failure of Business Strategy and Industrial Policy
Karel Williams, John Williams and Colin Haslam
0 85496 515 7
0 85496 516 5 pb

1992 – The Struggle for Europe

A Critical Evaluation of the European Community

Tony Cutler
Colin Haslam
John Williams
Karel Williams

BERG
New York / Oxford / Munich

Distributed exclusively in the US and Canada by
St Martin's Press, New York

First published in 1989 by
Berg Publishers Limited
Editorial offices:
165 Taber Avenue, Providence, RI 02906, USA
150 Cowley Road, Oxford OX4 1JJ, UK
Westermühlstraße 26, 8000 München 5, FRG

British Library Cataloguing in Publication Data

1992 – the struggle for Europe: a critical evaluation
of the European Community
  1. European Community countries. Economic integration
  I. Cutler, Tony
  337.1'42

ISBN 0–85496–596–3
     0–85496–666–8 pbk.

Library of Congress Cataloging-in-Publication Data

1992 – the struggle for Europe: a critical evaluation of the
  European community/Tony Cutler . . . [et al.].
        p.   cm.
  Includes bibliographical references.
  ISBN 0–85496–596–3
  1. European Economic Community. 2. European Economic Community
countries—Economic policy. 3. Monetary policy—European Economic
Community countries. I. Cutler, Tony.
HC241.2.A617 1989
382'.9142—dc20   89–35879

Printed in Great Britain by
Billing and Sons Ltd, Worcester.

Contents

Tables

Abbreviations

BOS	Basic Oxygen Steel-making process
CAP	Common Agricultural Policy
CBI	Confederation of British Industry
EAGGF	European Agricultural Guidance and Guarantee Fund
EC	European Community
ECU	European Currency Unit
EEC	European Economic Community
EFTA	European Free Trade Association
EMS	European Monetary System
ERDF	European Regional Development Fund
ERM	Exchange Rate Mechanism
ESCB	European System of Central Banks
ESF	European Social Fund
ETUC	European Trade Union Confederation
GDP	Gross Domestic Product
LRAC	Long Run Average Cost
M and A	Mergers and Acquisitions
METS	Minimum Efficient Technical Size
NATO	North Atlantic Treaty Organisation
NICs	Newly Industrialising Countries
NIESR	National Institute of Economic and Social Research
NTBs	Non Tariff Barriers
OECD	Organisation for Economic Co-operation and Development
PLC	Public Limited Company
PPP	Purchasing Power Parity

Abbreviations

RPI	Retail Price Index
SITC	Standard Industry and Trade Classification
SMMT	Society of Motor Manufacturers and Traders
STAR	Services de Télécommunication Avancée dans les Régions
TUC	Trades Union Congress
YTS	Youth Training Scheme

Introduction:
Not Really 1992

In the early 1980s, the political stock of the European Community was at an all time low. An enlarged Community had lost its way in a period of economic recession. There was low wrangling about budget contributions and reform of the Common Agricultural Policy (CAP). Brussels had a reputation for issuing pointless regulations; the Commission was pilloried in Europe's tabloid newspapers as the body which threatened the purity of German beer and the peculiarity of British ice cream. It all looked like something out of *opera buffa*. But by the late 1980s, the political stock of the European Community was riding high. In 1988 and 1989 no European quality newspaper was complete without a news story or feature about progress towards the 'single market' and the prospect of monetary union. The heavy and exhilarating libretto and score has become more like Wagner than *opera buffa*.

This transformation can be dated back to one turning point: the publication in 1985 of a European Commission White Paper, *Completing the Internal Market*. After twenty years of internal free trade without tariff barriers, the Commission now pressed the case for freer trade through removal of non-tariff barriers, such as border controls and technical regulations. This was all unpromisingly technical rather than visionary. But the Commission had carefully chosen an issue (maybe the one issue) which did not divide member states, and the Commission was then astute enough to get many of the 'single market' proposals enacted. The significance and effects of these largely symbolic changes were hugely hyped, and the Commission successfully created the impression

1

that it was building Europe. Once it had captured the political initiative, the Commission was determined not to let go. By mid-1988 the Commission believed it was possible to make progress on the difficult issue of monetary union, and in Spring 1989 the Delors Committee made detailed proposals to this end. If these proposals were to be enacted, they would constitute a major step in the direction of European unity.

By the time of the Delors report, reference to 1992 had become a tedious obsession and a substitute for thought by politicians, businessmen and economists. In the world of European big business, for example, very little of moment could happen without the obligatory reference to 1992. 'Preparing for the internal market in 1992' was an all-purpose excuse or justification to be used when mergers or joint ventures between European firms were announced, when multi-national companies decided to switch production from one country to another, or when a Japanese company decided to build a factory in the Community. Although 1992 does have some strategic implications, it is often irrelevant to such developments. Many of the economic conditions which will determine the shape and nature of the European economy in the 1990s were already in place before the 1992 programme was announced. As we argue in Chapter One, a definite pattern of trade and industrial location had already emerged in Europe by the mid-1980s. And Chapter Four shows that restructuring in European big business is conditioned by a variety of real forces which have little to do with 1992.

So, we have not written another book about '1992'. Instead, we aim to analyse the issues behind the 1992 programme and other EC policy initiatives, like regional and social policy or the plan for monetary union. We also want to set discussion of these policy issues in the context of a new and more realistic kind of economic and political analysis. More specifically, our aim is to explore two key issues which are largely ignored in the existing literature on the EC, which is narrowly technical and/or uncritically pro-European. Some economists, like Geroski (1988) and Neuberger (1989), have provided worthwhile critiques of 1992; but their criticism is inadequate because it unconsciously shares many of the premises and assumptions of the official pro-1992 literature. First, we wish to problematise the terrain of the current debate by identifying and dissecting the economic and political presumptions which underlie the 1992 programme and other EC policy initiatives. Our work here is an exercise in identification. Second, we wish to expose the implausibility of the official claims that the single market will be a source of economic gain and benefit for all Europeans, with regional policy compensating for any loss. Our work here is an exercise in criticism.

Our analysis of the political and economic *a priori* in current EC initiatives and policies is not confined to one 'philosophical' chapter. Analysis of the presumptions is integrated as a kind of counterpoint to our substantive economic and political analysis in successive chapters on trade in the EC; the 1992 programme; EC regional and social policy; business restructuring and competition policy; and current plans for monetary union. In all these policy areas, we detect the same underlying presumptions which fit together into a coherent liberal market *a priori*.

The 1992 programme, like existing EC regional policy and the plan for monetary union, is permeated with liberal market economic values. In an age when everybody is in favour of 'the market', it is important to be precise about what this means. As we have argued elsewhere (Cutler et al., 1986), in modern debates about economic policy and institutions, it is essential to distinguish between liberal market and liberal collectivist philosophies. The liberal market philosophy is to free the market on the grounds that this will produce optimality and economic efficiency. It is assumed that the economic and social consequences of unfettered market adjustments will be beneficial for most and tolerable for the minority, who necessarily but temporarily lose out. Liberal collectivists (and 'social market' socialists) start from a different premise: markets are indeed necessary and useful but need some degree of control, because unregulated markets produce a degree of economic instability and social division which is unacceptable in a political democracy, since their consequences endanger essential freedoms. The liberal collectivist response is to press for the minimum amount of state intervention necessary to reduce economic and social divisions and to stabilise the capitalist market system. It is the liberal market philosophy which dominates the 1992 programme, and there is precious little liberal collectivism in any major EC initiative; as we show in Chapter Three, even regional policy operates entirely in a liberal market framework.

Nevertheless, EC policy could not be described as liberal market economics in action because, for the Commission, the liberal market is mainly an instrument rather than a goal. For the President

3

and his cabinet, the transcendent objective is the unification of Europe. In all the many official texts on the economics of 1992, there is always a political sub-text: this programme is ultimately desirable because it promotes European unity and will strengthen Europe in global competition against Japan and the United States. The priority of the political objective was reasserted in 1988–9 when the Commission turned its energies towards promoting monetary union. The dominance of the political over the economic is indicated by the way in which the Commission is prepared to tolerate or promote a variety of economic anomalies. Most notably, the Commission has no credible plans to reform the CAP, which is indefensible because it raises Europe's agricultural prices above world market prices and thereby diminishes consumer welfare. Another anomaly arises out of the Commission's attitude to free trade, which is regionally desirable because it builds Europe but globally doubtful because it may weaken Europe as a bloc against Japan and the Newly Industrialising Countries: the Commission will countenance 'fortress Europe' if that is politically necessary.

In our view, a Europe built on liberal market foundations is neither desirable, nor stable. We argue that a liberal market Europe will harm all the poorer European countries whose economic policy choices will be constrained, and in many richer European countries it will hurt underprivileged working-class groups who will lose their jobs. In all our chapters we present economic arguments and evidence which document the illfare and disamenity which the 1992 programme and other EC initiatives will increase or sustain. Our central argument is that the Commission is simply wrong about the universal benefits of freer trade. It is true that orthodox economists come to very much more favourable conclusions about the consequences of free trade and EC policy. But orthodox economics has a strong bias in favour of liberal market solutions. Asking an economist to evaluate the 1992 programme is rather like asking a doting and defensive mother to comment on the conduct of her (ill-behaved) child: all we get is justifications and excuses.

In our work of criticism we aim to deconstruct the orthodox economic arguments and supporting evidence used in the official EC literature to justify 1992 and other EC policy initiatives. Each chapter considers a different policy issue or initiative, providing an organising principle for the book. The first chapter analyses the outcome of twenty years of intra-European trade without tariff barriers, while the second evaluates the gains which are supposed to result from the 1992 programme for removing non-tariff barriers. The third chapter considers whether regional policy does, or will, provide a defence against the consequences of market integration. Restructuring and the control of restructuring are considered in the fourth chapter, before, finally, we turn to consider plans for monetary union in our fifth and final chapter. The individual chapters ask and answer a series of master questions.

In Chapter One, the question is which nations have gained from free(r) trade in a tariff-free Europe. One of the premises of the 1992 programme is that everybody can and will gain from freer trade. We show that the results have been very different in a Community which contains one world-class economic power, Germany, with other member states whose economies are much weaker. There are strong centripetal tendencies within a Community where Germany, which has one-sixth of the EC 12 population, accounts for nearly 40 per cent of manufacturing output. The gains from freer trade have been mainly captured by West Germany. Ten of the eleven other EC countries have manufacturing trade deficits with West Germany, and these trade deficits set constraints on the adoption of expansionary, employment-creating policies elsewhere in Europe. The end result is a zero-sum game in which one country's gains have to be another's losses. In this case it is being played at a level below full employment, and the jobs are being transferred to Germany.

In Chapter Two we ask whether the 1992 programme will bring substantial benefits. After the publication of the 1985 *White Paper*, the Commission set up a large research project, on 'the costs of non-Europe', whose results were summarised for popular consumption in the Cecchini Report (1988). The headline claim was that 1992 means a significant gain in consumer welfare equal to 5–7 per cent of GDP plus 'millions of new jobs'. It is not difficult for us to show that these gains are both exaggerated and speculative. The direct economic benefits of removing NTBs are exceedingly small; the effect will probably be a once-and-for-all saving of less than 1 per cent of GDP. The larger bottom-line gains are obtained after the Commission's researches have piled one implausible conjecture upon another. We are sceptical of these conjectures and question whether European business will realise significant economies of scale after 1992, arguing that co-ordinated reflation will not happen.

At several points in Chapters One and Two, we argue that orthodox economics and the Commission's researchers not only get the
answers wrong but also ask the wrong questions. They are mainly
concerned with how trade increases consumer welfare by lowering
prices and increasing consumer choice; they do not give enough
attention to the impact of trade on producer welfare through job
loss in a Europe of mass unemployment.

The Commission endlessly reassures possible losers that its regional policy will compensate them. In Chapter Three we ask
whether the consequences of the market will be buffered by grants
from the structural funds? Our answer is that the existing regional
and social funds are completely inadequate to the task of dealing
with the existing imbalances between countries and regions within
the enlarged Community. This is partly because the funds are
simply too small and partly because the money goes on futile
infrastructural and training projects, which are ideologically sound
in liberal market terms but practically unlikely to redress large
inequalities in income. Worse still, the Commission's plans for
enlarging the regional and social funds will work, through the
matching grant system, to curb overall levels of government expenditure in poorer countries and to redirect public expenditure
onto acceptable liberal market objects. The rationale of more
regional aid, on these terms, is not assistance but liberal market
tutelage over the policies of poorer countries. These proposals for
regional policy are not an aberration. As we argue in Chapter Five,
the Delors plan for monetary union envisages a comprehensive
system of tutelage over the fiscal and monetary policies of poorer
countries.

In several chapters we note that there is a discrepancy between
the world as it is and the world as it is preconstructed in orthodox
economics and Commission policy. Nowhere is this clearer than in
the case of business restructuring, which is considered in Chapter
Four. Here, we ask: what form will restructuring take and who will
reap the benefits? In the official 1992 literature, restructuring is a
virtuous hypothetical mechanism which, in association with competition, delivers a supply side shock from which consumers benefit. Our conclusions, based on an analysis of existing patterns of
restructuring, are altogether more pessimistic. We believe that the
likely outcome of restructuring is a businessman's Europe where
existing centripetal tendencies are reinforced. In the second half of
Chapter Four, we ask whether EC policy can control restructuring.

We then demonstrate that the mergers and joint ventures which effect restructuring are largely unregulated by EC competition policy.

Bismarck observed 'Whoever speaks of Europe is wrong. It is but a geographic concept'. So far as the member states are concerned, Europe is becoming, but is not yet, a fact; the more rounded resonance is signalled by the way in which the description 'European Economic Community (EEC)' has been replaced by the more confident and comprehensive 'European Community (EC)'. In the texts of uncritical European enthusiasts, Europe is often described as a 'challenge'; that word figures in the title of the Cecchini Report and in the title of Michael Heseltine's (1989) recent book on Europe. In our view, Europe is less a challenge and more a struggle between contending economic concepts and political forces. All our chapters illustrate different aspects of that struggle, and in our fifth and final chapter, we consider some current political (mis)representations and visions of Europe's future. On the right, Mrs Thatcher's objections to loss of sovereignty do not represent a principled defence of national rights but rather an incoherent exercise in British chauvinism. Throughout the text we are concerned to distance ourselves from this chauvinism. We are not anti-European, nor (for all our criticism of German predominance) are we anti-German; we have tried to write a book which focuses on Europe's problems, rather than Britain's difficulties. On the left, we criticise the idea that a liberal market European programme can be accepted if it is supplemented with a 'social Europe' programme. We are sceptical about the efficacy of secondary redistribution and argue the case for alternative policies of direct intervention to ensure that centripetal tendencies are effectively combatted.

In some respects, the immediate political prospects are discouraging. Via monetary union, the Commission plans to deliver one more instalment of the liberal market solution. Because of the misrecognition of regional policy and unreal optimism about social Europe, the left is ill-placed to resist. But that does not mean that everything is settled. All the Commission's plans are riven with internal tensions, and contradictions and liberal market policies which promote inequality are bound to provoke political reaction. What will happen is a struggle to determine the current and future economic and political character of the European Community. The essential choice is between a Europe dominated by a liberal market philosophy and one which incorporates liberal collectivist and socialist elements. Our aim in this book is to reconceptualise the problem of Europe so that the political choices, especially for those on the left, become clearer.

Chapter 1
The German Co-Prosperity Sp

If academic economists are concerned with forecasts of the future, sceptical historians are concerned with inquests on the past. Economists now pose a master question about the future of the European Community after 1992: will freer trade, through removal of non-tariff barriers, bring substantial benefits to all European consumers? It is equally necessary to pose a rather different, historical question when the EC has been a free-trade community for the past twenty years: how has free trade operated to distribute benefits between the different member countries? The two approaches and questions are complementary. But, in our view, the historians' question is the logical starting point for any enquiry into the EC, and thus, our first chapter addresses that question before we turn in Chapter Two to confront the issues raised by the economists.

The two kinds of questions are answered from different sources using rather different ranges of techniques. The economists' question about the future requires simulation and modelling of outcomes. Much of their current discussion is in the form of a critique of the official European Commission projections of the benefits of 1992. The historians' question can be answered in a preliminary way by examining recent trade statistics. These official statistics are calculated separately by each member country of the EC. Our analysis of the division of benefits is, therefore, necessarily focused on the distribution of benefits between countries. This focus is a pragmatic necessity; it is not possible, from the available trade statistics, to calculate the division of benefits in any other way. But this focus has a variety of incidental benefits because the national

Table 1.1 Manufactured imports and exports (5–8) in current prices as percentage of GDP

	1970	1978	1981	1985
W. Germany				
Imports	12.0	14.3	16.9	19.3
Exports	17.6	21.1	24.0	27.7
UK				
Imports	12.8	18.8	15.8	20.0
Exports	14.5	19.6	15.9	17.1
Italy				
Imports	n/a	12.1	13.4	14.8
Exports	n/a	18.4	18.0	18.2
France				
Imports	n/a	12.5	14.2	15.6
Exports	n/a	14.6	15.9	16.7

Sources: *Eurostat Review 1977–85*, Series 1A; OECD, *Compatible Trade and Production Data Base*, 1970–85, Paris, OECD.

perspective illuminates important issues and mechanisms which have not been fully analysed in the existing literature on the European Community.

Trade and the division of output

To begin with, our question about the distributional effects of free trade has to be set in context. European trade is dominated by visible trade, which accounted for 81.6 per cent of all European trade in 1986. Many services which are significant in domestic economies are not traded internationally because they can only be consumed by those who are close to the point of production. This constraint does not apply to manufactured goods; consumers will not go to Germany to have clothes dry cleaned, but they will buy German automobiles. Our analysis, therefore, concentrates on the trade in manufactured goods, which accounts for four-fifths of the value of visible trade within Europe. Furthermore, it concentrates on the key component of that trade in manufactures, which is trade in SITC categories 5–8, i.e. manufactures with the exception of food, drink and tobacco. Category 5–8 trade dominates the trade in manufactured goods in Europe, accounting for 75–80 per cent of all European exports of manufactures. Thus, for the rest of the chapter trade in manufactures will be a shorthand for trade in category 5–8 products.

Table 1.2 The division of real manufacturing output[a] (5–8) and population between major EC countries

(a) output	1970		1977		1985	
	bill. ECU	%	bill. ECU	%	bill. ECU	%
Belgium	10.2	3.6	13.4	3.9	15.3	4.3
W. Germany	110.2	39.2	128.1	37.6	142.7	38.4
France	57.5	20.5	79.3	23.3	85.7	23.0
Italy	41.3	14.7	52.9	15.5	61.0	16.4
Netherlands	13.4	4.8	16.0	4.7	18.1	4.9
UK	47.2	16.8	50.3	14.8	47.8	12.8
EC 12		100.0		100.0		100.0
(b) population	1970		1977		1985	
	mill.	%	mill.	%	mill.	%
Belgium	9.638	3.2	9.822	3.1	9.858	3.1
W. Germany	60.651	20.0	61.400	19.6	61.024	19.0
France	50.772	16.8	53.145	16.9	55.170	17.2
Italy	53.661	17.7	55.955	17.8	57.141	17.8
Netherlands	13.032	4.3	13.856	4.4	14.488	4.5
UK	55.632	18.4	56.179	17.9	56.168	17.5
EC 12	302.847	100.0	313.910	100.0	321.407	100.0

[a]Output is net output or gross value added at constant 1975 prices and exchange rates.
Sources: *Eurostat Review 1977–85*, Series 1A; *European Economy*, Annual Report, no. 38, November 1988.

Trade in manufactures matters because it now has considerable weight and importance in economic activity. As Table 1.1 shows, category 5–8 manufactured exports and imports account for a substantial and growing proportion of national income in the four major EC economies; by the mid-1980s, manufactured imports accounted for 15–20 per cent of GDP, while exports accounted for 17–28 per cent of GDP.

There can be no doubt that international trade on this scale is an important driver of national prosperity in all the EC economies, and our question is about whether some countries benefit more than others from these trade flows. Before we turn to answer that question about dynamic effects, we can begin by observing the static division of manufactured output and trade between the different EC countries and how that has changed over the past twenty years.

Table 1.2 gives the distribution of EC 12 manufacturing output

Table 1.3 Manufactured exports (5–8) by country, as a percentage of EC 12 exports

	1960	1970	1980	1987
Belgium/Lux	9.6	10.4	9.2	8.6
Denmark	1.6	1.9	1.8	2.0
W. Germany	31.1	33.2	32.1	35.4
Greece	–	0.2	0.2	0.5
Spain	0.7	1.4	3.0	3.6
France	15.5	14.6	15.8	14.5
Ireland	0.2	0.4	0.9	1.4
Italy	8.3	12.0	12.7	13.9
Netherlands	6.5	7.6	7.0	7.1
Portugal	0.5	0.6	0.6	0.9
UK	25.8	17.7	16.1	11.9

Source: *Eurostat External Trade. Statistical Yearbook*, Series 6A, Table 7.

between the major EC countries, which accounted for more than 90 per cent of EC 12 output in 1970, 1977 and 1985. To establish a point of reference, the lower section of the table gives the relevant totals and distribution of EC population between the same countries.

Table 1.2 shows that West Germany has a dominant position in the European output league; this one country, with around 20 per cent of EC 12 population, has accounted for nearly 40 per cent of EC 12 manufacturing output over the past two decades. Comparisons are complicated because there were, over this period, significant shifts in national share further down the output league; between 1970 and 1985 Britain lost a 4 per cent share of EC 12 manufacturing output, while France and Italy together gained a similar share. But, leaving the complications aside, it is clear that France, Italy and Britain are also-rans in the output league. In terms of population, these three countries, each with 55 million plus citizens in 1985, are all nearly the equal of West Germany. But the French share of EC 12 manufacturing output is only just over half as large as the German share, while the Italian and British shares are even lower.

Germany is not only dominant in terms of output; it also has a leading role in European trade. As Table 1.3 shows, Germany's share of EC 12 manufactured exports is around one-third, and this share has tended to rise in recent years so that, by 1987, Germany's share was more than twice as large as that of any other country.

Germany's old challenger in the export trade was Britain, which

Table 1.4 Manufactured imports (5–8) by country, as a percentage of
EC 12 imports

	1960	1970	1980	1987
Belgium	11.0	10.2	10.1	9.1
Denmark	5.5	4.3	2.7	3.3
W. Germany	22.1	23.6	23.8	24.9
Greece	2.5	2.0	1.5	1.2
Spain	1.6	3.6	3.1	4.6
France	11.9	16.2	17.6	17.6
Ireland	1.7	1.4	1.7	1.5
Italy	9.3	10.5	11.0	11.6
Netherlands	12.7	11.9	9.7	9.7
Portugal	1.5	1.4	1.1	1.4
UK	20.0	14.9	17.5	16.1

Source: *Eurostat External Trade. Statistical Yearbook*, Series 6A, Table 7.

held a 26 per cent share of Europe's exports in 1960. However,
Britain's share has been halved in the past 25 years. Other countries,
notably Italy and Spain, have made gains in export share. But these
gains have been achieved on a modest initial base; the Italians have
gained 5.6 per cent in export share but started from an 8.3 per cent
share in 1960.

Equally significant, the EC's import trade in manufactures is
nowhere near as strongly centralised as the EC export trade. As
Tables 1.3 and 1.4 show, the German share of manufactured imports,
at 23 to 24 per cent, is substantially lower than Germany's share of
manufactured exports. The French and British import shares, at
around 17 per cent in 1987, are not so far behind. This difference
between the pattern of export and import shares is important because
it is a first indication of the trade imbalances which we shall analyse
later in this chapter.

While Germany plays the leading role in the export trade, it is
also the case that the German manufacturing sector is the most
export-dependent in the EC. The proportion of manufacturing
output exported has risen throughout Europe with trade liberalisation. But as Table 1.5 shows, the German manufacturing sector
started and continues at a higher level of export dependence than
the manufacturing sector of any other large European country. In
1970, the Germans exported just over one-quarter of their manufacturing output, and by 1985, the proportion was nudging one-
half. The percentage of output exported from France, Italy and

13

Table 1.5 Manufactured exports (5–8) as a percentage of domestic production in the four major EC economies

	1970	1978	1981	1985
W. Germany	26.1	36.9	40.8	47.6
UK	15.8	24.1	24.8	29.7
Italy	18.9	35.8	36.1	35.8
France	17.4	23.9	25.6	28.8

Source: OECD, *Compatible Trade and Production Data Base*, 1970–85, Paris, OECD.

Britain has always been significantly lower; in 1985, the simple unweighted average of the percentage of manufacturing output exported by these countries was 31.4 per cent.

How trade redistributes output

When the facts about output and trade are laid out in this way, we must begin to suspect that there is some connection between the export success of German manufacturers and the continuing pre-dominance of West Germany in the European output league. Surely, if the value of German exports were reduced, Germany's share of European manufacturing output would be smaller. But, it is necessary to be cautious about this kind of simple inference because the interconnections from, and repercussions of, trade are complex. For example, the effects of a reduction of German exports would partly depend on whether intra- or extra-EC sales were lost; only in the case of intra-EC sales is it reasonable to assume that lost German sales would mainly be claimed by other EC manufacturers. Or, to take another issue, it should not be assumed that German predominance in the output league is entirely the result of trade. For the past twenty years German levels of per capita income have been around 120 per cent of the EC average, and domestic affluence must work autonomously inside Germany to sustain a high value-added manufacturing sector. In any case, quite apart from these complications, an exploration of how trade contributes to German success is not enough. It is as, or more, important to ana-lyse whether and, if so, how other EC countries lose through trade.

To resolve these issues about the national distribution of the benefits from trade within the EC, it is necessary to do more than observe the elementary facts. We must also provide a simple analysis of how manufacturing trade operates centripetally to re-

Table 1.6 National shares of EC extra-European manufactured (5–8) exports

	1960	1970	1980	1987
Belgium/Lux	6.2	5.3	5.0	5.1
Denmark	1.7	2.6	2.2	2.7
W. Germany	30.7	34.8	34.9	39.6
Greece	–	0.2	0.4	0.4
Spain	–	1.8	3.2	3.4
France	15.9	15.9	16.1	14.3
Ireland	–	–	0.4	0.8
Italy	8.1	11.8	13.2	14.2
Netherlands	4.5	4.5	4.1	4.4
Portugal	0.6	0.8	0.6	0.6
UK	32.1	24.1	19.6	14.4

Source: *Eurostat External Trade. Statistical Yearbook*, Series 6A, Table 7.

inforce Germany's predominance by redistributing output partly at the expense of other European countries. Before analysing other countries' losses, we will first analyse German gains. In both analyses we must distinguish between extra- and intra-European trade, which have different transfer effects.

In extra-European trade, Germany wins an output boost by taking an increasing share of European exports. German manufacturers have the capability to survive and prosper against Japanese and American competition in highly competitive world markets. As Table 1.6 shows, the German share of extra-European trade has increased by nearly 10 points over the past 25 years to reach a level of about 40 per cent. Thus about two-fifths of all EC manufacturing exports to the rest of the world are accounted for by Germany.

This boost is well worth having because, as Table 1.7 shows, the value of extra-EC exports is not much smaller than the value of tariff-free intra-EC exports; in 1987, extra-EC exports accounted for 43 per cent of all EC exports. And this boost is probably not obtained directly at the expense of other European countries. If BMW or Mercedes gain an American market sale, that will not necessarily be at the expense of Renault or Fiat; the likely loser is a non-European producer like Cadillac or Honda. But the German gains in extra-European markets do have European repercussions. Through success in world export markets, the Germans tap a powerful stimulus which has multiplier effects on their rate of domestic output growth, and that allows them to achieve what

Table 1.7 Intra- and extra-European shares of EC manufactured (5–8) exports

	Intra-European %	Extra-European %
1960	36.1	63.9
1970	50.6	49.4
1980	54.3	45.7
1987	56.7	43.3

Source: *Eurostat External Trade. Statistical Yearbook*, Series 6A, Table 7.

they regard as adequate growth rates without recourse to expansionary domestic fiscal and monetary policies. The European policy environment might be much more expansionary if the Germans were compensating for world market failure rather than graciously adapting to success.

The pattern of intra-European trade is even more interesting. The balance between extra- and intra-European trade changed with the creation of the free trade community in the 1960s. As Table 1.7 shows, since 1970 intra-EC manufactured exports have accounted for the larger and the faster growing part of all European manufactured trade. This expanding intra-European trade does involve direct transfers of output; the success of BMW and Mercedes in the European executive and luxury car markets is partly achieved at the expense of Renault and Fiat. Despite this, the overall picture on intra-EC export shares is one of relatively stable country shares; there have been nothing like the 10 per cent or more share shifts that have occurred in the extra-European trade. As Table 1.8 shows, Germany does not claim an increasing share of intra-European exports. But because the volume base of German intra-European exports is much larger than those of its competitors, a *pari passu* expansion of German exports in line with the European total drives up the value of the manufacturing trade deficits which other European countries run with Germany.

On intra-European trade, the key indicator of output transfer is the deficit which every other established EC manufacturing country (except Ireland) runs with West Germany. As Table 1.9 shows, each one of these countries now imports more manufactures from Germany than it exports to Germany, and the resulting deficits represent a (net) transfer of output to Germany at the direct expense of these other countries; the size of the deficit in millions of ECU

Table 1.8 National shares of EC 12 intra-European manufactured exports (SITC 5–8)

	1960	1970	1980	1987
Belgium	15.4	15.8	13.0	11.1
Denmark	1.4	1.3	1.5	1.5
W. Germany	31.4	32.5	30.2	32.2
Greece	–	0.3	0.5	0.5
Spain	–	1.1	3.0	3.7
France	18.0	15.8	16.3	14.7
Ireland	0.5	0.6	1.3	1.8
Italy	8.5	12.5	12.8	13.7
Netherlands	9.9	10.4	9.2	9.2
Portugal	0.4	0.5	0.7	1.3
UK	14.3	9.1	11.4	10.0

Source: Eurostat External Trade. Statistical Yearbook, Series 6A, Table 7.

represents the amount of gross output (or sales) which was transferred by each country to Germany in 1974, 1981 and 1987.

This process of output transfer through trade is not a recent consequence of economic recovery and cyclical upswing in the 1980s: as Table 1.9 shows, all the other established EC manufacturing countries were in deficit on their manufactured trade with Europe as long ago as 1974. The aggregate transfer of sales (or gross output) value to Germany is now very large; in 1987 it amounted to 34 billion ECU. Whatever assumptions one cares to make about prices and exchange rates, the value of the transfer has undoubtedly increased in real terms over the 1980s; in current prices there was a 2–3 times increase in the ECU deficit with West Germany between 1981 and 1987.

If Germany gains output from intra-EC trade, other countries lose output, and the most obvious loser is Britain. If EC and world trade is the context in which German manufacturing strength manifests itself, it is also the context in which British manufacturing weakness manifests itself. Britain's record on extra- and intra-European trade is a kind of inverted image of the German record. The British cannot survive in open, competitive markets; when the going gets tough, the British response is retreat. Thus, in extra-European trade, Britain has a record of ruinous share loss; the British share of EC exports fell from 32 to 14 per cent over the twenty-five years after 1960. In intra-European trade, Britain loses because, at the end of a period of steady deterioration towards the

17

Table 1.9 Matrix table of manufacturing trade balances[a] for eight of the EC 12 countries

(a) 1974 manufacturing trade balances (mill. ECU)

Reporting country	W. Germany	France	Italy	Netherlands	Belgium/Lux	UK	Ireland	Denmark
France	-2,450.7	–	-88.5	-294.7	-853.1	202.5	47.7	91.4
Belgium/Lux	-525.4	626.0	187.7	641.4	–	-535.2	17.2	216.1
Netherlands	-2,063.2	161.7	-8.6	–	-651.0	-218.8	52.7	109.3
W. Germany	–	2,313.9	1,331.2	2,035.6	447.2	1,575.0	140.7	874.6
Italy	-1,268.2	-419.1	–	-72.4	-140.4	168.5	42.9	54.4
UK	-1,439.4	7.6	-50.2	-125.1	247.2	–	501.2	185.4
Ireland	-128.9	-38.9	-34.1	-36.2	-23.3	-606.4	–	-16.6
Denmark	-864.5	-72.9	-50.3	-107.6	-128.3	-196.4	15.5	–

(b) 1981 manufacturing trade balances (mill. ECU)

Reporting country	W. Germany	France	Italy	Netherlands	Belgium/Lux	UK	Ireland	Denmark
France	-5,637.9	–	-711.9	-817.6	-2,266.8	957.4	17.5	-0.9
Belgium/Lux	-2,008.6	1,802.4	517.7	-317.1	–	230.9	-59.9	180.4
Netherlands	-1,366.2	777.0	23.9	–	-35.3	-141.0	-45.0	112.0
W. Germany	–	5,306.5	1,607.7	3,249.5	1,199.6	3,499.4	85.3	1,006.7
Italy	-1,076.4	1,274.5	–	42.5	-533.0	726.4	6.7	117.7
UK	-3,606.4	-828.6	-508.4	85.4	-1,314.6	–	1,658.8	76.1
Ireland	-87.6	40.3	-16.7	-7.1	2.2	-1,754.0	–	32.7
Denmark	-965.9	-22.5	-117.0	-90.9	-278.5	-1.6	54.8	–

(c) 1987 manufacturing trade balances (mill. ECU)

Reporting country	W. Germany	France	Italy	Netherlands	Belgium/Lux	UK	Ireland	Denmark
France	-8,986.1	–	-2,852.2	-1,127.4	-2,096.9	2,165.4	-601.3	201.6
Belgium/Lux	-3,872.9	4,069.2	1,637.7	593.9	–	544.6	-240.7	445.3
Netherlands	-5,684.7	1,400.3	962.7	–	-24.2	1,111.8	-200.2	233.3
W. Germany	–	9,176.5	3,312.0	6,013.7	3,202.6	10,290.2	-204.0	2,403.7
Italy	-2,820.0	3,573.8	–	-407.5	-1,244.6	1,998.1	-233.0	348.4
UK	-10,802.7	-1,584.3	-2,122.4	-1,534.4	-655.6	–	–	-179.1
Ireland	205.1	637.7	196.8	128.8	133.8	-686.1	–	5.1
Denmark	-2,328.5	-119.1	-354.3	-215.5	-439.3	82.1	-29.5	–

[a]Surpluses and deficits are calculated from the NIMEXE analytical tables where merchandise is classified into 'chapters'. Results approximating to SITC 5–8 can be obtained by adding together surpluses and deficits in chapters 1 to 27 and deducting this total from the overall surplus/deficit of chapters 0 to 99.

Source: Eurostat External Trade. Analytical Tables, Series 6C.

end of the 1980s, it was running a deficit on manufactured trade with every other EC country, except Ireland. In 1987 the total British deficit on manufactured trade with other EC countries was 16.9 billion ECU. No less than two-thirds of that deficit was accounted for by the 10.8 billion ECU deficit with West Germany. But as Table 1.9 shows, Britain also now runs significant deficits on manufactured trade with France, Italy and the Netherlands.

Britain's trade problems have recently attracted increasing attention and concern. The overall current account deficit in the second half of the 1980s was increasing at an alarming rate as the oil surplus continued to decline and the deficit on manufactured trade increased remorselessly. In 1988 the British deficit on trade in manufactures was £17.3 billion, and the overall current account deficit was £14.7 billion or 3.5 per cent of GDP. The logic of this situation is that the British economy of the 1990s will be trade-constrained and payments-crisis prone, as it was, in more favourable circumstances, for thirty years after the Second World War. But in discussion of the recurrence of the old British problem, the new European dimension has been neglected or ignored. The fact is that Britain has had a deficit on manufactured trade with Europe since 1973, and as Table 1.10 shows, this deficit has grown enormously in recent years and is consistently larger than Britain's deficit on manufactured trade with the world as a whole.

By 1988, Britain had a deficit on European trade in manufactures of £19.6 billion, which was larger than the £17.3 billion deficit on manufactured trade with the rest of the world (including Europe). The implication of this, of course, is that British trade in manufactures with the rest of the world (excluding Europe) was in surplus. All, and more than all, of Britain's deficit in manufacturing trade arose from trade within the Community.

Within Europe, the disparity in manufacturing performance between Britain and West Germany is such that the intra-European transfer of output is increasingly concentrated along the one axis between these two countries. The matrices in Table 1.9 show that the British deficit with Germany is now larger than that of any other country, and Britain accounts for an increasing proportion of the rest of Europe's trade deficit with Germany; the British share of the larger rest of Europe deficit has risen from 16.7 per cent in 1974 to 31.6 per cent in 1987. The British case is obviously the most dramatic. But it would be wrong to focus exclusively on Britain's loss, when virtually all the other EC countries are in deficit, and the

Table 1.10 The UK commodity trade balance, manufacturing trade balance and manufacturing trade balance with other EC members, 1975–88 (£mill.)

	Trade balance[a]	of which: manufacturing[b]	of which: EC members
1975	−4,233	+3,660	−376
1976	−5,422	+4,403	−232
1977	−3,647	+5,501	−239
1978	−3,548	+4,026	−1,445
1979	−5,664	+1,653	−2,607
1980	−2,409	+3,641	−1,723
1981	−170	+2,905	−3,000
1982	−1,420	+198	−5,004
1983	−5,417	−4,849	−8,049
1984	−8,194	−6,308	−8,863
1985	−6,635	−5,806	−9,599
1986	−13,188	−8,245	−10,925
1987	−14,164	−9,944	−11,133
1988	−24,937	−17,314	−19,584

[a]Trade is merchandise trade SITC 0–9.
[b]Manufacturing is SITC 5–8, excluding food, drink and tobacco.
 The figures are on an OTS basis seasonally adjusted and are crude trade balances.
Source: Department of Trade and Industry, *UK External Trade by Area*, Commodity Analysis.

overall European deficit on manufactured trade with Germany was five times greater than that of Britain alone in the mid-1970s and remains three times greater in the 1980s. All the other European countries lose from intra-European transfer of output, some more so than others.

An illuminating way of comparing the losses of different countries is to show them in relation to population. This can be done if we measure the per capita value of manufactured imports from Germany and the per capita size of the deficit on manufactured trade with Germany. Table 1.11 presents the results of such a calculation and shows that Britain, the country with the largest absolute deficit, is by no means the biggest per capita loser.

With deficits per head in the range of 350 to nearly 500 ECU, the Netherlands, Belgium/Luxemburg and Denmark have the highest per capita transfers of output to West Germany. The UK and France are towards the rear with very much smaller deficits of 150–200 ECU per capita. The more general drivers of output

Table 1.11 Per capita deficits on manufactured trade with Germany and
per capita imports of manufactures from Germany, 1987

1987	Deficit/ surplus with Germany (mill. ECU)	National population (mill.)	Deficit per capita ECU	Imports from Germany per capita ECU
France	−8,986.1	55.632	−161.5	500.5
Belgium/Lux	−3,872.9	10.240	−378.2	1,670.4
Netherlands	−5,684.7	14.615	−388.9	2,034.5
Italy	−2,820.0	57.355	−49.2	337.7
UK	−10,802.7	56.810	−190.2	376.6
Ireland	205.1	3.543	+58.0	303.1
Denmark	−2,328.5	5.127	−454.2	924.9

Sources: Eurostat External Trade. Analytical Tables, Series 6C; *European Economy*, no.
38, November 1988, Annual Economic Report, 1988–9.

transfer would thus appear to be cultural similarity, contiguity to
Germany and high levels of income per capita. It is these factors
which account for the very high per capita level of manufactured
imports from Germany in the Netherlands, Belgium/Luxemburg
and Denmark; the Dutch import of German manufactures per
capita is five times as high as the British import. Cultural difference,
distance and relative poverty help to explain why all the south European
countries have low per capita imports and deficits with Germany.

The transfer of employment, policy constraints and policy choices

Having analysed how trade redistributes output, we can now turn
to answer the next question as to whether and, if so, how these
transfers matter. The simple direct answer to this question is that
output transfer in manufacturing matters because output takes
employment with it. This result is inevitable when in western
Europe nearly 70 per cent of net output in manufacturing is claimed
by labour in the form of wages. As we have argued elsewhere in a
discussion of cyclical fluctuations (Williams et al., 1989), if value
added or net output falls significantly, then there is little headroom
for labour's share to expand, and formidable pressures soon develop to cut the size of the manufacturing workforce. Thus, in the
two recent recessions after 1973 and 1979, the pattern was one of
reductions in the workforce which are more or less commensurate

Table 1.12 Germany's employment gain from its 1987 manufacturing surplus with the rest of Europe

(1) Surplus with the EC 12	34,200 mill. ECU
(2) Domestic Value Added from this surplus 34,200 × 0.73[a]	24,966 mill. ECU
(3) Average compensation per wage/salary earner	22,957 ECU
(4) Employment gain from (2) 24,966 mill. ECU ÷ 22,957 ECU	1,087,500

[a]This deflator was applied to take out the import content of the extra output obtained from having a surplus with the rest of the EC. The deflator is a cautious estimate based on the ratio of all merchandise imports to manufacturing gross output.

Sources:
(1) *Eurostat External Trade. Analytical Tables*, Series 6C (Luxemburg, 1988).
(2) UN, *National Accounts. Main Aggregates and Detailed Tables*, 1985, Tables 3.51 and 4.2 (UN, New York, 1987).
(3) *Eurostat National Accounts*, ESA Series 2C, 1970 to 1987 (Luxemburg, 1988).

with the fall in output in different advanced countries.

This insight into the mechanics of cyclical fluctuation can be developed so that it is possible roughly to quantify the scale and extent of employment transfer which is implied by the surplus of Germany with other European countries, or by the deficits of individual countries with Germany. There are two essential steps in this calculation: first, the amount of net output or value added which has been gained or lost must be estimated; and second, to obtain an estimate of the number of jobs gained or lost, the average wage in the country which gains or loses is divided into the 'wages fund', which is determined by the share of value added that labour claims. Table 1.12 gives a detailed step-by-step calculation which shows that the German surplus with the rest of Europe represents a gain of 1.1 million jobs for Germany. When wage rates are low in other EC countries and each ECU of value added therefore creates more jobs outside Germany, the same amount of value added outside Germany would, of course, sustain a substantially larger number of jobs.

Table 1.13 analyses the other side of the two-way transfer process. It uses the same procedures to estimate the job loss which Britain suffers as a result of its deficit with Europe. The bottom line is that the British deficit with the rest of Europe represents a job loss of 0.77 million.

Table 1.13 Britain's employment loss from its 1987 manufacturing deficit with the rest of Europe

(1) Deficit with EC (12)	15,990 mill. ECU
(2) Domestic Value Added loss from this deficit 15,990 × 0.70[a]	11,193 mill. ECU
(3) Average compensation per wage/salary earner	14,474 ECU
(4) Employment loss from (2)	773,000

[a]The factor of 0.70 applied to correct for the import content of domestic output lost by Britain's manufactured trade deficit. The deflator is a cautious estimate based on the ratio of all manufactured imports to manufacturing gross output. (Based on Sources 2 and 3)

Sources:
    (1) *Eurostat External Trade. Analytical Tables*, Series 6C (Luxemburg, 1988).
    (2) Department of Trade and Industry, *British Business*, Imports of Principal Products of Division 2 to 4, 1987 (DTI, Sept., 1988).
    (3) *Census of Production PA 1002*, Table 1: Manufacturing Gross Output Divisions 2 to 4 (HMSO, 1987).

The results of these rough calculations are broadly consistent with the large observed differences between the sizes of the manufacturing workforces in Germany and Britain. With roughly similar populations and workforces, the West German manufacturing sector sustains 7.2 million manufacturing jobs at the highest wage rates in Europe; the British manage 5 million jobs at wage rates which in real purchasing power terms are probably half to two-thirds of West German levels. Nevertheless, many economists would refuse to take these calculations seriously because they are counterfactual calculations which presuppose that when the value added is gained by Germany (or lost by Britain) everything else stays the same. These economists would argue that other things are not equal or, anyway, that other things should not be equal for losers. If one country is losing output and employment through trade, the appropriate response would be for that country to choose more expansionary fiscal and monetary policies which boost domestic output and employment. In that way, some economists would argue, nobody need lose from trade, and all countries will benefit from higher levels of output and employment. Against this, we would argue that, in Europe now, the economists' favourable outcome is considerably more remote and unreal than our own worst-case counterfactual calculations.

Inside the EC, the deficits with Germany not only transfer

output and employment from all the other countries, these deficits also establish a constraint on the adoption of expansionary monetary and fiscal policies which would re-employ underutilised or unemployed domestic resources. As is argued in the concluding chapter, these constraints will, unless there are strong countervailing policies, be greatly increased as Europe moves to monetary union.

Even in advance of monetary union, in each European country which loses through trade, the crucial question is whether the deficit on manufactured trade with Germany is large enough to push the current account into deficit. If the current account is in or near deficit, then expansionary fiscal policies become problematic, even if national governments are prepared to accept devaluation. Outside the Scandinavian countries, those who are unemployed are maintained on doles which are well below the average wage. Re-employment of unemployed workers at or near the average wage will usually increase the demand for imported (German) manufactures dramatically and aggravate any current account deficit.

Table 1.14 demonstrates that this kind of trade constraint is already a reality in Europe in the late 1980s. It shows that all the European countries are in, or near, current account deficit and that their deficits on manufactured trade with Germany are a major contributory cause. The UK already (1988) looks to be payments-constrained; with the current account deficit running at 3.5 per cent of GDP, any attempt to expand output and employment would result in a terminal payments crisis. Other countries are more favourably positioned. But that does not mean their currencies and current accounts would hold up if their governments embarked on a reflationary experiment. It should be remembered that, in the early 1980s, Mitterrand's reflationary experiment in France was cut short by speculation against the franc which anticipated a deterioration in the French trade position.

The transfer of output and employment to Germany and the creation of constraints on the expansion of employment and output elsewhere in Europe would not matter if the other European countries were at or near full employment. But, as Table 1.14 shows, Europe in 1987 was far from full employment, however that condition is defined. And it should be emphasised that 1987, in unemployment terms, was a good year which was probably at or near a peak of cyclical activity after six years of continuous recovery from the recent slump. Towards the end of that recovery there

Table 1.14 Trade constraints in EC countries, 1987

Country	(1) Current account surplus/ deficit (mill. ECU)	(2) Surplus/ deficit as percent of GDP	(3) Surplus/ deficit on intra- European manufactured trade (mill. ECU)	(4) Deficit on manufactured trade with Germany (mill. ECU)	(5) Unemploy- ment rate %
Belgium/Lux	2,528	3.5	1,545	–3,873	11.1
Denmark	–2,563	–3.0	–4,196	–2,329	n/a
W. Germany	39,009	4.0	40,165	–	6.2
Greece	–1,114	–3.4	–2,726	n/a	n/a
France	–4,555	–0.3	–19,648	–8,986	10.6
Ireland	343	1.3	518	205	n/a
Italy	–885	–0.1	4,824	–2,820	11.8
Netherlands	2,923	1.7	–5,776	–5,685	9.6
Portugal	555	1.8	–1,672	n/a	7.0
Spain	n/a	–0.3	–5,074	n/a	20.1
UK	–3,620	–0.6	–16,329	–10,803	10.3

Sources:

(1) *Eurostat Balance of Payments, Quarterly Data*, 2–4, 1988; *Economy and Finance*, Series 2B.
(2) *European Economy*, No. 38, November 1988, Annual Report 1988–9, Table 42.
(3) *Eurostat External Trade. Statistical Yearbook*, Series 6A, Table 7.
(4) *Eurostat External Trade. Analytical Tables*, Series 6C.
(5) OECD, *World Economic Outlook*, December 1988.

were 13.9 million unemployed in 1987 in the 11 EC countries (excluding Germany). In this context of trade constraint plus mass unemployment, intra-European trade serves as a mechanism for passing the parcel of unemployment to weaker countries who are then in no position to eliminate unemployment through expansionary policies. To that extent, trade guarantees the persistence of mass unemployment which can be characterised as the social price which other European countries must pay for keeping their deficits with West Germany inside manageable limits. Apologists for free trade believe that the Community owes its prosperity to being a free trade area; but a study of the pattern of trade reveals that the Community under free trade is a German 'co-prosperity' sphere in which prosperity is divided unequally.

The paradox is that Germany appears to derive relatively modest benefits from its advantage in trade. There is a massive transfer through trade of employment to Germany, but the German economy does not have full or nearly full employment. In 1987, the German unemployment rate was 6.2 per cent; that is better, but not hugely better, than the unemployment rate in France or Britain. As we have argued, the transfer of employment is the consequence of the transfer of output to Germany. But this transfer of output is achieved without any obvious centralisation of production. As Table 1.2 showed, the German share of EC 12 manufacturing production has not been increasing; over the past twenty years, Germany's share has been constant at just under 40 per cent. Closer examination of the evidence shows that these paradoxical effects are due to the slow growth of German manufacturing output. And, on our interpretation, this slow growth of output can be attributed to restrictive fiscal and monetary policies inside Germany. The gains from manufacturing trade allow Germany the luxury of cautious policy choices which offset the expansionary employment and output results which would otherwise be expected.

Table 1.15 shows that real manufacturing output in Germany over the past two decades has increased more slowly than in France and Belgium, which have not enjoyed the same success in trade transfer terms. Between 1970 and 1986 the real net output of all these countries, with the striking and marked exception of the UK, grew more rapidly than the real net output of German manufacturing. These results are not so surprising when production growth is affected not only by export success, but also by the level of import penetration. Furthermore, trade balance does not completely explain increases or decreases in a country's production share over time, because the rate of growth of the total domestic market in each country is another important influence on domestic output growth. The evidence reviewed in the next few paragraphs suggests that, in the case of West Germany, the beneficial effects of export success are countervailed by above average levels of import penetration and by below average rates of domestic market growth.

Within the various countries of Europe, import penetration is not a function of national manufacturing strength; it is, jointly, a function of consumer tastes and the extent of national measures to block imports from Japan and the Newly Industrialising Countries. German consumer tastes are as, or more, cosmopolitan than those elsewhere in northern Europe, and their national government is less ruthless than the French or Italian government in blocking imports like Japanese cars. Consequently, as Table 1.16 shows, for the past fifteen years import penetration in Germany has consistently been above the level of import penetration in the UK, France and Italy; the import share of the German domestic market for manufactures

Table 1.15 Real net output growth in eight EC countries since 1970 (1970=100)

	Belgium	Luxemburg	Denmark	Germany	Greece	France	Netherlands	UK
1970	100	100	100	100	100	100	100	100
1975	118.8	100.7	115.1	104.3	143.1	123.3	110.2	101.7
1980	138.9	111.8	132.3	119.6	180.1	142.2	124.8	96.8
1986	159.2	135.3	152.7	130.1	181.6	140.0	136.7	101.4

Note: The above figures relate to gross value added at market prices at 1980 prices in national currencies.
Source: Eurostat National Accounts, ESA, 1988; *Economy and Finance*, Series 2C.

Table 1.16 Import share by value of the domestic market for manufactures in four major EC countries, 1970–85

	1970	1978	1981	1985
West Germany	19.5	28.4	32.6	38.7
UK	14.2	19.0	24.7	33.2
Italy	16.3	26.9	29.7	31.3
France	16.2	21.1	23.6	27.4

Note: The domestic market for manufactures is calculated as production minus exports plus imports.
Source: OECD, *Compatible Trade and Production Data Base*, 1970–85, Paris, OECD.

has, for example, usually been at least 5 per cent higher than the import share of the British market. It is often assumed that Britain is the 'warehouse economy' of Europe. But that epithet could with more justice be applied to Germany, whose factory economy is partly dedicated to covering the cost of German imports.

The German trade surplus indicates that German manufacturers succeed triumphantly in this task. But that success does not allow rapid growth, because German manufacturers must live with slow rates of home market growth, and around one-half of their output is still sold at home. In countries like France, Italy and Britain where two-thirds of the domestic manufacturing sector's output is sold on the home market, the rate of domestic market growth is the dominant influence on the rate of output growth sustained by the national manufacturing sector. And there can be little doubt that the French and Italian domestic markets have grown faster over the past twenty years. Table 1.17 gives a comparison of growth in the real domestic market for manufactures in the four major EC economies. Nominal domestic market growth is calculated by subtracting exports and adding imports to the value of domestic production; real growth is then obtained by applying the relevant Retail Price Index deflator to the nominal totals for each country.

Over the whole period, the rate of domestic market growth in Germany was very much slower than the rate of growth in France and Italy; between 1970 and 1985 the German market increased by some 10 per cent in real terms whereas the French and Italian markets increased by one-third. As usual the British occupy their reserved place at the bottom of the table, suffering an actual decline in the real domestic market between 1970 and 1985. But until the 1979–81 recession, the rate of growth of the German domestic

Table 1.17 Growth in real domestic manufacturing markets in four EC
countries (index 1970 = 100)

	1970	1978	1981	1985
West Germany	100	103.3	109.2	109.1
UK	100	108.9	87.1	90.0
Italy	100	108.1	119.1	133.7
France	100	127.8	132.5	133.7

Note: The domestic market values for manufactured goods have been deflated by
national RPI to obtain real values. ISIC Division 3 was used as an approximation to SITC 5–8.

Source: OECD, *Compatible Trade and Production Data Base*, 1970–85, Paris, OECD;
and OECD, *World Economic Outlook*, December 1988.

market was actually below that of Britain's.

Slow rates of domestic market growth, and the persistence of
unemployment, can be attributed to Germany's maintenance of
domestic fiscal and monetary policies which are generally restrictive. It is not possible to encapsulate the policy stance of the Federal
Government and the Bundesbank in one or two simple measures.
Budgetary stance is inherently difficult to measure in a federal
system where the Länder have substantial budgets at the state level.
Monetary policy is perhaps easier to measure but more difficult to
interpret, because the targeted variables changed with monetarist
fashions in the 1980s, and most monetary authorities were con-
spicuously unsuccessful in controlling their targeted variables. The
commitment of the Bundesbank to monetary restraint is illustrated
by the maintenance of high real interest rates. For example, in the
period 1974–9, Germany was the only one of the seven largest
OECD economies with a positive average real short-term interest
rate. Over the more recent period of 1980–5, German short-term
real interest rates averaged 4.3 per cent against 2.5 per cent in the
UK; the long-term average rates are 4.8 per cent and 2.1 per cent
(OECD, *World Economic Outlook*, December 1988).

Trade-constrained, deficit-running countries have no choice
about adopting restrictive policies; this point does not need to be
laboured in a country like Britain where interest rates were raised
dramatically in 1988 and 1989 as the current account deteriorated.
As a surplus country, Germany can choose to adopt expansionary
or restrictive policies. The Germans choose restrictive monetary
and fiscal policies under a kind of division of labour where responsibility for maintaining what they regard as adequate growth rates is

entrusted to their manufacturers. The settlement seems to be that the federal government and the Bundesbank keep policy restrictive and let German manufacturers organise their own reflationary salvation by expanding their export sales in European and world markets. And, within Europe, Germany's enterprise-led reflation then works by deflating somebody else's economy. It is ironic that the Commission (in a prevaricating way) now proposes co-ordinated European reflation. As we argue in the next chapter, co-ordinated European reflation is a scenario which is highly unlikely, even though a section of the European left is fervently hoping for its implementation. Meanwhile, what has mostly escaped notice is that the Germans are already operating their policy of go-it-alone reflation through enterprise action; inside Europe, this kind of reflation operates on a basis which holds Germany (and every other country) well short of full employment. It would be as well for all of us to confront the inadequacy of this real-world outcome before we turn to dream of alternatives.

Why European trade is not identified as a problem

The transfer of output and employment through intra-European trade is an issue which has largely been ignored in mainstream research and political discussion. The German trade surplus is sometimes deprecated, but the distributional mechanisms and the results of intra-EC trade are little analysed. Fundamentally, this is because the problem of intra-European trade is not within the area of the visible in the discourse of orthodox economics, and not within the area of the sayable in current EC politics. For a variety of discursive or pragmatic reasons, economists and politicians have been unable or unwilling to make the kind of analysis that has been offered in this chapter. The economists' misconceptions and the politicians' silences go unchallenged because trade has not yet produced an obvious centralisation of production with full or overfull employment in Germany. In the final section of this chapter we aim to define and challenge the prevailing (mis)conceptions, and we shall begin by considering the treatment of trade in economics before turning to examine the political reasons for concentrating on the actual and potential benefits of trade.

The idea that trade might be a zero-sum game, with the gains appropriated by one party, is anathema to orthodox economists. In this sense, as it is expressed in the Padoa-Schioppa report:

> The most basic analysis of the effects of international trade in goods
> and services has not changed in its essentials since Ricardo expressed
> the principle of comparative advantage in the early nineteenth cen-
> tury. Countries trade because they are different; each country special-
> izes in activities in which it is relatively efficient, or which use
> intensively its relatively abundant resources. This specialization raises
> the efficiency of the world economy as a whole and produces mutual
> benefits to the trading nations. (Padoa-Schioppa, 1987, Appendix A,
> p. 118)

And 'although new developments in the analysis of international
trade', such as the recent stress placed on economies of scale and
oligopoly, 'have modified this view, the insights from conventional theory remain important' (ibid). Since our concern is with
the broad principles and implications of the economists' approach,
attention will be concentrated on the basic comparative cost argument.

The economists presuppose that international trade, according to
the principles of relative price and comparative cost, yields benefits
for all participants. Orthodox economists start from the theoretical
demonstration that two (or more) countries *would* both gain if they
specialised through trade in categories of production where their
relative advantage was greater (or their disadvantage was less).
Economists then make a substantial leap to the assumption that
international trade *is* governed by the principle of comparative
advantage even though the relevance of the two-country, two-
commodity model is questionable in a world which includes corporate actors and non-price competition. The doctrine of comparative advantage thus functions as a kind of interpretative
rhetoric which rationalises whatever pattern of trade is observed or
predicted and provides an assurance that everything is for the best
in this best of all possible worlds. Thus, Pelkmans and Winters
(1988) review British performance in manufacturing trade and
observe that Britain's share of the total of French, German and UK
exports in sectors like aerospace and computers is around 35 per
cent, whereas in a sector like motor vehicles it is around 15 per
cent. Their interpretation is that Britain has a revealed comparative
advantage in these sectors and that removal of non-tariff barriers
under the 1992 programme will lead to further specialisation and
gains for Britain and her European partners. As Pelkmans and
Winters (1988, p. 111) half-heartedly admit, the alternative – and in
our view more plausible – explanation is that the British export

share is highest in areas of sheltered production, subsidies and public procurement, which have combined in some high-tech sectors of British manufacturing to sustain a production base which generates exports. In this case, the removal of non-tariff barriers in 1992 is more likely to lead to the erosion of the British production base and losses for Britain.

According to comparative advantage, specialisation realises gains in consumer welfare. But clearly international trade also leads to relocation of industry which dislocates producer welfare. British consumers gain from access to German cars or Italian sweaters, while producers in the Midlands lose jobs because their cars or knitwear are no longer required. However, this is not a major problem for orthodox economists because they are committed to the sanguine assumption that displaced resources will not be unemployed for long. If this assumption is valid, then the dislocations arising from trade are all part of a larger beneficial process of structural change in advanced economies. Just as in each national economy, the producers of motor vehicles put the producers of horse-drawn vehicles out of business in the early twentieth century, so, internationally, the more capable producers of motor vehicles should put the less capable producers out of business in the late twentieth century. The problem, of course, is that it is not at all clear that the resources displaced by trade will be effortlessly re-employed in the less successful European economies, which are now characterised by mass unemployment and trade constraints. In the European economies which lose from trade, those who are fortunate enough to retain their jobs do derive some benefit from having the choice of a wide range of imported goods. But cheap and attractive consumer goods in the high-street shops are no consolation to those who are unemployed and cannot afford these goods.

The reassuring syllogisms and assumptions of orthodox economics have always been questioned by a dissident minority. Unorthodox economists like Culbertson (1986) propose absolute cost theories of trade. Orthodox theory suggests that trade will take place and be mutually beneficial, even if one country is all-around more efficient. This is because the degree of comparative advantage (or disadvantage) will differ for different goods and so encourage countries to specialise. Absolute costs theory, which is generally dismissed as a recurrent heresy, asserts that the trade advantage rests with the country with lower costs until the other country (or countries) takes, or is forced to take, steps to reduce its costs. On this view, international trade involves unfair competition because advanced countries cannot meet the challenge of competition from countries whose manufactured exports are sustained by low wages and government subsidies. The end result of international trade is a reduction in living standards in the advanced countries; the only way in which high-wage countries can meet unfair competition is through wage cuts, and if labour market rigidities prevent sectoral wage cuts, then currency depreciation will in due course impose an across-the-board reduction in living standards. This interpretation explains part, but not all, of the current pattern of international competition. Absolute cost explains some of Japan's initial success, as well as the more recent gains of the Newly Industrialised Countries (NICs) through trade. And if Europe were not protectionist against imports from the NICs, the absolute cost theory would doubtless explain a much larger part of extra-European trade. But absolute cost does not explain the pattern of intra-European trade. According to absolute cost theory, European manufacturing production should be migrating to the low-wage Mediterranean countries. But only one of these countries, Spain, is increasing its share of European manufacturing production and exports, and even those gains are relatively modest. Within the terms of this theory, it can only seem paradoxical that Germany, the highest-wage country in Europe, maintains and strengthens its dominant position.

The radical economists are no more successful than their orthodox colleagues in explaining the pattern of intra-European trade. That is because they remain within the problematic of a discourse which does not admit, and therefore cannot conceptualise, national differences in the capacity to organise production as a source of competitive advantage. Some economists, such as Geroski (1988), do emphasise a rather different consideration, the heterogeneity of consumer tastes, as a major reason why Europe will never be a single market like the USA. In washing machines, the French prefer top loaders, the Germans insist on long-wash programmes which get clothes cleaner, and the Italians are happy to buy slow-spin machines which are unacceptable in Britain. The importance of these differences is easily overrated. When manufacturers can easily build variant machines for different markets and the consumers in each national market do not all have the same tastes, heterogeneity of consumer tastes does not substantially block the growth of intra-European trade. Heterogeneity of national producer capability is a more important consideration because these differences drive the growth of unbalanced trade flows. In white goods, all over Europe, German manufacturers succeed up-market by selling over-engineered quality products, while the Italians dominate a mass market which is concerned with features and price competitiveness. If these facts are not generally taken on board by economists, that is because economics does not provide the conceptual tools for analysing national differences in producer capability.

National differences in organisational capacity surface in empirical research like the NIESR case studies of kitchen cabinets and metal goods (Daley, Hitchens and Wagner, 1985; Steedman and Wagner, 1987) which observe the contrast between German efficiency and British disorganisation of production. But these differences cannot be analysed using orthodox micro-economic theory, which has a cake-mix concept of production where factor inputs tagged with prices are combined in a simple single-process, single-product operation. Significantly, the exemplary NIESR studies cannot entirely escape this framework and end by putting considerable emphasis on the higher quality of the labour force in Germany. Their restrictive concept of production prevents economists from seeing that, for example, decisive cost and quality advantages can be obtained by reorganising the flow of work between manufacturing processes so as to minimise stocks; this point is invisible because economists do not appreciate, as Toyota managers do, that stocks drive costs through the employment of unnecessary, indirect labour in multi-process, multi-product manufacturing operations (see Williams et al., 1989a). This failure to conceptualise differences in national capacity to organise production makes it even more difficult to conceptualise the determinants of those differences. As a discourse, economics aims to provide a general theory of capitalist calculation within which national institutional differences are suppressed or accommodated only through their influence on prices and costs. Some years ago, we sketched an institutional explanation of British manufacturing performance where institutional variables, like the role of financial institutions, were the crucial conditions (see Williams et al., 1983). In orthodox economic analysis, these institutional considerations barely figure.

Partly because the discourse does not analyse the heterogeneity of producer capability, the orthodox economic analysis of tariffs and the effects of removing tariffs is deficient. This is a crucial issue, given the concerns of this chapter, which has reviewed the consequences of twenty years of trade without tariffs inside the EEC. In economics tariffs are the work of the devil because a tariff is a tax on consumers which featherbeds inefficient producers to the general detriment of allocative efficiency; blanket hostility to tariffs carries over into scepticism about the advisability of allowing exceptions in special cases such as infant industries. The orthodox condemnation of tariffs is, in its own terms, excessive; under conditions of oligopoly and imperfect competition, the allocative effects of moving from one sub-optimal outcome to another are usually unclear. Furthermore, the condemnation fails to discriminate between the very different welfare and locational effects of tariffs in various circumstances; more specifically, it fails to distinguish the different effects which arise when inward investment is, or is not, blocked. In the advanced countries, when tariffs are raised or maintained, inward investment is usually allowed. And most of the force is removed from the orthodox condemnation if, in a world of heterogeneous producer capabilities, inward investment is freely allowed. Under these conditions, if import blocking tariffs are maintained around a substantial market, the likely consequence is a relocation of producer firms from countries with superior organisational ability who will choose to claim their share of value added and profit by producing behind the tariff barrier. This is how and why the Americans came to Europe before and after the Second World War, and it is why the Japanese are now coming to Europe. In so far as firms do migrate and replace or improve the inferior performance of domestic firms, the welfare losses sustained through tariffs are likely to be very small.

From this point of view, import blocking tariffs can be seen as a positive instrument which secures some kind of rough balance between the location of production and the size of the local market; any substantial market behind tariff barriers will be served by the local production of domestic and multi-national firms. The general outcome under free trade conditions without tariff barriers is likely to be different and inferior in terms of producer welfare in the receiving country. The incentive to move production to the market is much weaker and will only apply in the special circumstances where heterogeneity of consumer preferences dictates production of variant lines close to each market. More generally, under free trade, manufacturing firms are not blocked or penalised if they choose to supply local markets with direct exports from their

Table 1.18 German investment in manufacturing at home and abroad in 1987–8

	Gross fixed capital formation in manufacturing (bill. DM)	Direct investment in manufacturing abroad (bill. DM)
1987	67.1	2.98
1988	70.1	7.90

Source: Economic Statistics Department, Bundesbank, Frankfurt (Communication 31 May 1989).

national home base. Concentration of production at home base is an attractive option for most firms. In their home economy, firms negotiate a familiar institutional environment, and they benefit from short organisation and communication lines as well as established suppliers. Inside a free-trade area, differences in producer capability will only be slowly equalised by the relocation of production facilities or the transfer of management with superior capability. The likely consequence is unbalanced trade flows, job transfer and the creation of trade constraints.

The intra-European transfers of output and employment have already been analysed. We can now add the point that these transfers arise because, with tariffs removed, German manufacturers have been understandably reluctant to manufacture outside Germany in any other country of the EC; the German strategy within this free-trade area is 'Made in Germany' and sold abroad by a wholly-owned distributor. This interpretation is partially confirmed by Table 1.18. This takes German gross fixed capital formation as a measure of German investment in domestic capacity. The scale of such investment can then be compared with the scale of German investment in overseas capacity through purchase of foreign companies and direct investment in overseas subsidiaries.

The figures in Table 1.18 show that in 1988 the German investment in domestic capacity was nine times larger than investment in manufacturing abroad. Of course, these figures measure flow rather than stock; they do not show the balance between German overseas and domestic capacity. We have been unable to obtain figures on the overseas production or capacity of German manufacturing. But it is exceptional for 'household name' German firms to have large-scale manufacturing operations elsewhere in Europe, and the few exceptions to this rule do not always form encouraging precedents.

When transport costs are low and there are no content regulations requiring a given percentage of local content to be embodied in the production of a good, the non-German branch factories can be assembly operations where the local (non-German) content is very low. This is increasingly the case in the best publicised example of German manufacture elsewhere in Europe. In 1986, VW bought a 75-per-cent stake in SEAT, the market leader in the Spanish car market, which up to that point had concentrated on meeting local demand with modified FIAT designs. VW bought SEAT because it wanted extra assembly capacity in a low-wage area; the aim was to move production of VW's small car, the Polo, out of the giant Wolfsburg factory. The Spanish content on this tranche of SEAT's capacity is likely always to be limited because the Spanish factory's role is to assemble kits of German parts, and the rest of SEAT's operation now seems to be going the same way. When VW took over in 1986, SEAT was a company on the road to full manufacture; its newly launched Ibiza light car was the first SEAT to contain a newly designed engine which SEAT itself manufactured. But this trend is being reversed under VW's current strategy. Early in 1989, VW announced a £3.3 billion investment which would develop SEAT as a third Euro brand, to back up Volkswagen and Audi (*Financial Times*, 22 January 1989). Although the body designs of future SEATS will be unique, the cars will use VW engines and transaxles, many of which will apparently come from VW's German factories. On the Volkswagen and Audi brands, VW already operates a comprehensive policy of commonality which extends to low-value items like door locks and steering column switches. As that policy is extended to SEAT, VW's German suppliers will gain useful extra business at the expense of their Spanish counterparts. By the mid-1990s, Spanish screwdriver manufacturers might be the major local beneficiaries of VW's takeover of SEAT.

Economics is a discourse burdened by a relentlessly optimistic *a priori* about the inevitably beneficial effects of free trade. Europe's politicians are more realistic. For example, whatever economists may recommend, it will be surprising if Europe's politicians were entirely to open Europe to free imports from Japan and the NICs. The politicians are aware that this kind of free trade would result in the transfer of output and employment to the Far East. By contrast, inside Europe, the 1992 programme is explicitly about the creation of even freer trade through the removal of the remaining non-tariff barriers to intra-European trade. As we argue in the next chapter, the inconsistency arises because free trade inside Europe is seen as an economic instrument which can serve the higher political goal of European unification. And the Euro-politicians give this mission such priority that they choose to ignore or distort the available evidence about what free trade without tariffs has achieved and what freer trade with non-tariff barriers might deliver. The discussion of the effects of removing non-tariff barriers is reserved for the next chapter. At this point, however, it can be noted that the 1992 literature sponsored by the Commission fails to confront the effects of free trade over the past twenty years.

None of the official 1992 reports contain any analysis of how gains from trade have been (or will be) divided between countries. The Commission prefers to discuss the problem of backward and peripheral regions, which is much safer politically because almost all of the EC countries have backward regions. It is more regrettable that the Commission chooses to avoid the evidence about intra-European trade patterns and flows. Their most outrageous claim is that intra-industrial trade only changes the fine detail of specialisation and 'usually entails only reallocation [of resources] within the same industry or even within the product range of the same firm' (EC, 1988, p. 139). Partly for this reason, at a national level 'intra-industrial trade, in which similar but different products are traded (e.g. France and Germany sell to and buy from each other motor car.), has few reallocative and redistributive effects' (ibid, p. 140). This assumption is built into the Commission's partial equilibrium model of the micro-economic benefits of 1992, and it serves to rationalise the claim that over the past twenty years 'the redistributive effects empirically observed (notably following the abolition of tariff barriers within the EEC) have been relatively slight' (ibid, p. 140).

The Commission's comfortable assumption about balanced intra-industrial trade is flatly contradicted by the available evidence. The German success in capturing the gains from trade is built on a narrow front of success in motor vehicles and capital goods; partly as a consequence, on a European basis, intra-industrial trade in both categories is thoroughly unbalanced. Table 1.19 shows the size of the German surplus in the four relevant SITC categories since 1970. Transport machinery and equipment always earns at least three-quarters of the total German surplus. And transport machinery's share of the intra-European surplus is even higher; in the early and

Table 1.19 German trade surplus by industrial class since 1970 (mill. ECU)

SITC	Intra-European	Extra-European
5 chemicals	2,932	8,848
6 manufactured goods by material	4,535	5,645
7 transport machinery & equipment	27,845	39,075
8 manufactured goods miscellaneous	341	–545
	35,653	53,023

1986 SITC 7 surplus = 78.1 of Germany's intra-European surplus and 75.5 per cent of Germany's total (intra- and extra-European) surplus.
Source: Eurostat External Trade Statistics, Yearbook, Series 6A, Table 7.

mid-1970s, it was at or above 85 per cent. Much of the class 7 intra-European surplus is earned through the export of German motor cars, whose value per unit sold is, of course, much higher than that of any other consumer durable. Most of the German export sales in Europe are at the expense of other European car manufacturers. The result is an unbalanced pattern of trade flows in cars, the very sector which the Commission holds up as an exemplar of balanced trade.

As Table 1.20 shows, in terms of unit volume the trade in cars between France and Germany is balanced, but in every other case the flows are unbalanced. And because the Germans specialise in the production of larger, more expensive cars, the disparities in terms of value are even more pronounced.

The Commission's cavalier treatment of the economic evidence on trade shows the strength of the European political imperative to get and keep the European show on the road. But all around Europe, national governments and official agencies with different political values and constituencies also studiously avoid the issues raised by trade within the German co-prosperity sphere. In this respect it is instructive to consider the British Department of Trade and Industry's memorandum submitted to the Aldington Committee (House of Lords, 1985) which blew a semi-official whistle about the link between British manufacturing decline and emerging payments problems. The statistical appendix in this memorandum presents various tables on the composition and history of the

Table 1.20 Intra-European trade flows in motor cars, 1988 (unit volume)

Reporting Country	Exporting Country			
	UK	France	Italy	W. Germany
UK	–	−70,629	−53,963	−305,865
France	+70,629	–	+150,309	−35,380
Italy	+53,963	−150,309	–	−109,747
W. Germany	+305,865	+35,380	+109,747	–

Source: SMMT, *World Automobile Statistics Yearbook*, 1989, Table 74.

British balance of payments which illustrate the shift from manufacturing surplus to deficit. But none of the tables breaks down the manufacturing trade balance into European and non-European components. From the DTI memorandum it was quite impossible to see that the cause of the British manufacturing trade deficit was Europe in general and Germany in particular. We can only speculate about why it was decided to present the evidence on British trade in such a curious way. Our conjecture would be that it was to avoid presenting evidence which might encourage the atavistic British hostility to the EC and/or raise again the issue of the terms of British membership, which has only been decently buried in the 1980s. As for the arguments and evidence summarised in this chapter, the official British response may well be that it is tantamount to starting the Second World War all over again because this interpretation must have the political effect of ranging most of the rest of western Europe against the Germans.

That would be quite mistaken, and it would certainly misrepresent our position and intention. In our view, there are no good arguments for ignoring or suppressing the evidence about the division of gains from trade. The Brussels justification about 'building Europe' should not be accepted uncritically even in Brussels; the economic and political content of European integration does matter. And it is hard to see how Europe can be built securely on a foundation of evasions about the consequences of intra-European trade. The current pretence is that the single market is above politics and that the economic imbalances which arise from trade can be ignored. That is futile because 'Europe' is politics carried on at a supra-national level, and the transfer of output and employment through intra-European trade is likely to become a political issue. Our evidence and arguments could be appropriated by a populist or chauvinist politics of national grievance to whip up hostility to German manufacturing and the Germans without offering any constructive solution. Alternatively, the same evidence could be integrated into an internationalist left politics which establishes the case for new forms of EC and national government intervention to redress the consequences of trade. The latter would represent our standpoint, and the best way for the left to prepare is through a sober realism which pushes trade up the agenda of issues which have to be confronted.

Meanwhile, when our arguments and evidence are still unfamiliar, it is worth insisting that they are neither anti-European nor anti-German. A generalised anti-European position is now economically and politically obsolete; apart from other more positive considerations, the EC 12 countries have no geo-political alternative to living together in a dense network of economic and political relations. That is why even British opposition to membership of the EC has died the death; it is impossible, even if it were desirable, to recreate our trade with Commonwealth countries or to recreate the Sterling Area. The Mediterranean countries which have since joined and the EFTA group who are worried about exclusion, equally know that the EC is the only club in town. It is exactly because Europe in general must be all our futures that we must examine and criticise the current particular set of economic and political arrangements. And that can be done without being anti-German. There should be no question of blaming the Germans for their manufacturing success or hoping for their failure. If the Germans were reduced to the British level of incompetence in manufacturing, that might solve the problem of intra-European trade balance but at the cost of weakening Europe as a whole. We need instead to give some priority to nurturing German industrial standards in other areas of the Community. Meanwhile, the point we should emphasise is that the intra-European free-trade system has had consequences which are both against the interests of non-German members and not entirely in the interests of Germany. The other states should complain that German trade success creates problems for them, and the Germans should reflect that they derive constrained benefits from a trade success which allows their authorities to persist with unduly restrictive internal policies.

Finally, we need not apologise if our arguments and evidence lead us to question the liberal market and free trade. The observed pattern of unequal gains from trade is only disillusioning for pro-market ideologues who believe that free markets invariably produce outcomes which are efficient and equitable. The rest of us are not dismayed to find that particular markets do not deliver these outcomes and that new forms of intervention are required to redress the consequences. Of course, it is not easy to devise intervention which is adequate in scale and content; in Chapter Three we demonstrate how the EC's existing social and regional policy is both inappropriate for, and inadequate to, the task of redressing the inequalities inside Europe. But the first step is to change the problem definition, and that is what this chapter has tried to do. The next step is to scrutinise carefully the claims put forward for the specific 1992 programme, and that is our object in the next chapter.

Chapter 2
The 1992 Programme

The abolition of tariffs twenty years ago did not create a single, integrated market. A variety of non-tariff barriers continued to impede the free movement of goods, capital and labour within the EC. These non-tariff barriers, or NTBs, include a variety of border controls and checks, differences in national technical regulations and standards, government preferences for domestic producers in public procurement, exchange controls, fluctuating exchange rates and differences in national tax regimes. Under the 1992 programme, the EC proposes to remove many of these barriers and promises to create a single integrated market. Our analysis of the consequences of (non-tariff) free trade in the EC over the past two decades makes us sceptical about the benefits of yet freer trade over the next decade. If the NTBs are significant barriers to trade, it would seem probable that their removal is likely to reinforce the dominant position of West Germany in intra-European trade.

The 1992 programme was originally formulated in a 1985 EC White Paper. In this chapter we begin by analysing its political and economic aims and character; we also point to some substantial inconsistencies and contradictions. After this preliminary analysis, we turn to examine the Commission's large claims about the benefits of 1992 which have already been criticised by independent economists such as Geroski (1988) and Neuberger (1989). The Cecchini Report (1988) assumed that the NTBs were a significant impediment to free trade and claimed that their partial removal would yield a substantial increase in consumer welfare. Against this, we argue that Cecchini's methods and procedures are dubious and that the Commission's sectoral research studies on 'the costs of non-Europe' provide an inadequate basis for the claims. Our conclusion is that the direct benefits of 1992 are small and the indirect benefits are uncertain. When it proclaims the benefits of 1992, the Commission is guilty of self-delusion and self-serving optimism. This point is established mainly by critical argument within an orthodox economic framework. As we argued in the first chapter, that framework is itself in some respects inadequate. For that reason, in the final section of this chapter, we examine the implications of 1992 for producer welfare and show that 1992 means job loss.

The aims and character of the 1992 programme

As a preliminary, it is necessary to emphasise that the 1992 programme for removing NTBs and creating a single market is an economic instrument which serves the political end of European unification. This is understandable if we remember that the Commission's (self-appointed) task is to guard and promote the cause of European unity. Through the late 1950s and the 1960s, the original six member states seemed to be making rapid progress in this direction. But the process of unification lost momentum in the decade or so from the mid-1970s, which was a period of oil shocks, sharp slow-down in world trade and doubling of the Community's membership. The 1985 *White Paper* on the completion of the internal market was economically an attempt to get the unification process rolling again. What we are given is an economic text with a powerful political sub-text. The economic-cum-political development of the EC is presented as a teleology which will now triumphantly culminate in political unification: 'just as the Customs Union had to precede Economic Integration, so Economic Integration has to precede European Unity' (EC, 1985, p. 55). For the Commission, European unity has a self-evident transcendent value which requires no justification; the only question is about how the process of unification can best be advanced.

In the late 1960s and early 1970s the emphasis had been on monetary union. Although the European Monetary System was created, none of the larger plans were realised because monetary union awkwardly and directly threatened the prerogative of national governments over monetary and fiscal policy. In this period the NTBs did not figure prominently in the Commission's strategy, and occasional attempts to attack government preferences were completely ineffectual; as the Commission now admits (Cecchini, 1988, p. 18), 1971 and 1977 EC directives designed to open up public contracts to foreign firms were ignored by national governments. But priorities and tactics changed in the early 1980s. The 1985 *White Paper* rests on the assumption that removal of NTBs can play a strategic role in promoting European unity. It argues that the original Treaty of Rome 'specifically required not simply the abolition of customs duties as between member states but also the elimination of quantitative restrictions *and of all measures having equivalent effect*' (EC, 1985, p. 5, our emphasis). Priorities shifted partly because the Commission made a political calculation that it was possible to make progress on this issue. And whatever one may think about the transcendent value of European unity or about the practical effects of removing NTBs, the EC undoubtedly pressed the issue in a way which was exceedingly astute. Once it had been decided that the immediate objective was to be the clearing away of the NTBs, the necessary instruments to give effect to the policy had to be put in place. In particular, two substantial tactical political difficulties had to be confronted and overcome: first, under the EC rules of the game in the early 1980s, any initiative on the NTBs could have been blocked by veto in the Council of Ministers; and second, anything which got past the Council of Ministers was likely to bog down in endless multilateral negotiations with twelve established networks of vested interests.

To begin with, it was therefore essential to abolish the requirement for unanimity in the Council of Ministers before any of the Commission's proposals could be enacted. The Single European Act (SEA) was designed to solve this problem. This measure, which was finally approved in July 1987, substituted qualified majority voting in the Council of Ministers over a wide range of issues. The Commission had always had the power to issue directives – binding Community-wide decrees which have the force of law – as long as they secured the unanimous approval of the member states in the Council. Indeed, under the EC's very peculiar constitution, the bureaucracy is, in some important respects, effectively the legislature, since proposals for legislation can only originate in the Commission. But after the Single European Act, the Commission could prepare directives without risking the possibility that they could be blocked in the Council by the veto of one member state. Thus, the Commission believes that it can now eliminate most of the frontier barriers and the accompanying paperwork by simply ordering the close-down of border posts between member states. Frontier controls will not be abolished overnight by legislative fiat, but the Commission's increased power under the SEA gives it a much stronger negotiating position *vis-à-vis* the member states. At the same time, the Commission does not want to engage in protracted negotiations on the removal of each NTB, so it has also adopted a strategy which is designed to neutralise some NTBs in a way which makes negotiation unnecessary.

The 'Cassis de Dijon' ruling of the European Court forced the West Germans to admit a French liqueur which did not meet the relevant German regulations; the principle was that a good 'lawfully produced and commercialised' in any one country of the Community could be freely transported and sold in other member countries without being modified, tested, certified or renamed. In the 1985 *White Paper*, this already recognised principle was elaborated into a new principle of 'mutual recognition' of technical standards for manufactured goods; the new principle is essentially that if, for example, a washing machine or television set is legally sold in any EC country, it is impossible to block its import into another EC country on the ground that it does not meet local technical regulations. In this way, the power of national technical standards to block imports could be undermined, even if there is no Europe-wide agreement on an international standard. Mutual recognition is represented as 'the first tool the Commission has . . . to ensure the free flow of goods' (EC, 1988d, vol. 4, p. 135). Each national government still has the obligation to protect public health, safety and the environment, but even in these areas the process of harmonisation is much simplified. Instead of directives laying down detailed specifications, there is a simple outline of the principal features products must have ('Essential Requirements'), and compliance with these 'European Standards' guarantees access to all European markets. A directive of 1983 on Mutual Information already obliges member states to notify the Commission of any proposed technical regulation and empowers the Commission to delay the implementation of such national regulations by one year (ibid., and EC, 1988, pp. 10–12).

In financial services the emphasis is on a different principle, but the same minimalism is at work. 'Home country control' provides for financial institutions to be primarily supervised by the relevant authority in their home country. 'Mutual recognition' then applies to allow these institutions to market their products throughout the

Community. The member states themselves have undertaken (at agreed dates) to remove exchange controls and to strive towards 'approximation', rather than harmonisation, of VAT rates.

The EC had good political reasons for focusing on the removal of NTBs; if the issue was pressed shrewdly, partial removal of NTBs could be brought within the realm of the politically possible. But it must also be emphasised that the 1992 programme had a distinctive economic content. The various measures to remove the NTBs were in the end merely instruments for facilitating and accelerating the wider operation of what was seen as the fundamental driving force: the market itself. A great deal was left to the operation of market forces to produce both European unity and European economic efficiency. It was assumed, mostly implicitly, that these forces were fundamentally benign in their operation. All of this made the whole 1992 programme much more acceptable to those member governments which were influenced by the philosophy of liberal market economics.

In the 1980s general ideas about the benefits of increased competition, deregulation and extending market relations have become a *motif d'espérance* in economic policy. The influence of such ideas now extends far beyond their traditional political constituency on the radical right; they influence the actions of socialist governments in Spain and New Zealand, as well as the attitudes of communist economic reformers from Hungary to China. The 1992 programme is the Commission's attempt to exploit this opportunity. In the *White Paper*, removal of NTBs is explicitly justified as a reform which will make European reality more like liberal market theory. Thus, the *White Paper* argues that the removal of NTBs will serve the purpose of 'ensuring that the market is flexible so that resources, both of people and materials and of capital and investment, flow into the areas of greatest economic advantage' (EC, 1985, abridgement, p. 2). While, in financial markets, 'decompartmentalisation . . . should boost the economic development of the Community by promoting an optimum allocation of European savings' (ibid., abridgement, p. 19). Furthermore, the principle of mutual recognition can be plausibly represented as a policy of deregulation because it emasculates existing national regulations without necessarily imposing a superstructure of supra-national regulation. By the mid-1980s removal of NTBs was a liberal market idea whose time had come.

If at first sight the programme appears internally coherent and governed by liberal market concepts, it also contains major anomalies. The Commission's commitment to realising the liberal market utopia was always qualified and contradicted by distinctive political aims and calculations. Thus, the *White Paper* includes supplementary political themes which would be suppressed in an orthodox liberal economic discourse and also edits out elements of the liberal market programme which are politically unacceptable or problematic.

To start with, in the official account the programme has a function in the competitive economic struggle between the world's major power blocs. In this respect a strand of Euro-chauvinism runs through the 1985 *White Paper* and many other Commission documents. The Commission's geo-political premise is that Europe cannot take its rightful place as a great power bloc if it has a weak manufacturing economy which cannot meet the challenge of Japanese and American competition. The fear is that 'the Community might lose ground to its main trading competitors' (EC, 1985, abridgement, p. 14). According to the *White Paper*, the 1992 programme for removing NTBs will simultaneously secure the liberal economic aim of freer trade (within Europe) and the geo-political aim of strengthening European manufacturing (against the rest of the world). There is, nevertheless, an inevitable tension between the two sets of objectives. For liberal market economists, free trade is a world principle, whereas for Euro-chauvinists, free trade is a regional European principle which should not be extended to include Japan and the NICs. And the contradictions become acute if the liberal market medicine fails to cure the disease of Euro-sclerosis; in that case the Euro-chauvinists might quite reasonably prefer non-liberal economic instruments, such as active industrial policy, as a means of strengthening Europe. It is not yet clear what will emerge in terms of the EC's trading relationships with countries which are outside the Community, although the signs are that, at a minimum, quantitative controls will continue (on an EC rather than national basis) against the Japanese: the Japanese certainly think so. But the point is that these issues and contradictions could not arise in a purely orthodox liberal economic discourse where the sole aim must be to increase consumer welfare through setting the market free; the accumulation and enlargement of political power is not a legitimate objective in liberal market economics.

If politics added the ingredient of Euro-chauvinism to the 1992 programme, politics also edited out a whole series of issues, most notably monetary union and the reform of the CAP. Monetary unification was certainly an issue to be dodged. A single market logically requires a tight monetary alliance, or a monetary union, which pegs the value of all 12 member-state currencies. In the *White Paper* this was the aim that dare not speak its name because tight alliance would require the subordination of national monetary policies to the requirement of maintaining a set exchange rate. It was prudent to keep monetary policy off the agenda for 1992 because it was an issue which was likely to provoke acrimonious debate and blocking vetos in the Council of Ministers. The Commission preached a politically edited and moderated version of the liberal market gospel.

The most glaring exception to the liberal market ideology, however, arises from the treatment of the Common Agricultural Policy (CAP). From the outset the Treaty of Rome had set out the central aim of the CAP to 'ensure a fair standard of living for the agricultural community' (Article 39). The method that has been adopted is to guarantee incomes by the use of a comprehensive system of price support: Community producers are protected against competition from agricultural imports from third countries by the setting of a 'threshold price' for imports, and duties are applied to such imports to bring their price up to the threshold level. National intervention agencies are obliged to purchase surplus output at a guaranteed intervention price. The result has, in sharp contrast to liberal market precepts, been a major exercise in import substitution. Table 2.1 uses the example of Australia to demonstrate the extent to which third-country shares of EC markets have fallen.

The cost of the CAP is funded from the Community budget, and as EC agricultural prices have been set consistently above the level of world prices, the cost of the policy has been substantial. The commitment to purchase surplus output makes the cost especially severe since it carries with it the need for large expenditures on storage and disposal. As we shall see in Chapter Three, attempts to reform the CAP have resulted in some modifications, so there is no longer a completely open-ended commitment to purchase surplus output at a guaranteed price. Nevertheless, the basic framework remains in place for most agricultural commodities.

An assault on the CAP formed no integral part of the 1992 programme. And yet as the summary below indicates it would be difficult to imagine a set of arrangements which could be more

Table 2.1 Australian exports of selected products to the EC (kilo tonnes)

	1966–8	1982–3
Beef and Veal	26.7	8.9
Barley	7.0	0.0
Sugar	400.0	0.0
Butter	57.1	0.3

Source: M. Roarty, 'The impact of the CAP,' National Westminster Bank Review, February 1987, p. 16.

diametrically opposed to the avowed objectives of 1992 than are those for the CAP.

Principles of the Internal Market	CAP
Removal of non-tariff barriers force down market prices	Administered prices
Rationalisation leads to survival of only the most efficient enterprises	Prices set at a level allowing inefficient units to survive
Removal of physical controls	Quotas used to restrain growth of output
Consumer gain promoted by price reductions	Consumers pay prices well in excess of prevailing world market prices

The internal market programme envisages the removal of obstacles to trade, so that market forces promote the alignment of prices over the EC, yet the CAP works through administered prices set by a process of *political* decision-making at Community level. The internal market programme sees the increase in competition as generating increased economic efficiency via 'restructuring' which will leave only the most efficient production units, yet CAP prices are set at such a level that the least efficient producers can survive. The internal market programme is designed to remove barriers which function as 'equivalents' to tariffs and quantitative restrictions, yet

51

Table 2.2 EC prices as a percentage of world prices for selected agricultural commodities

Product	1975–6	1976–7	1977–8	1978–9	1979–80
Common Wheat	124	204	216	193	163
Rice	137	166	128	157	131
Barley	117	147	206	225	161
Sugar	109	176	255	276	131
Butter	320	401	388	403	411
Skimmed Milk	266	571	494	458	379

Source: M. Roarty, 'The impact of the CAP,' *National Westminster Bank Review*, February 1987, p. 21.

in the attempt to restrain budget expenditure, CAP quotas have been re-introduced. And whilst the Commission sees the gains from the removal of NTBs as mostly occurring through the promotion of 'consumer welfare' by enabling consumers to purchase goods at lower prices, the CAP means, as Table 2.2 shows, that these same consumers pay prices for food well in excess of world food prices.

Given the starkness of the contrast between the 'principles' of the internal market and the CAP, one might have expected that the reform of the CAP would receive extended critical attention in the 'official' 1992 literature. This is not, however, the case. The issue is not raised at all in Cecchini's book, and in the more developed argument, 'The Economics of 1992' (EC, 1988), it is covered in less than two pages. If large exceptions to the basic liberal market ideology could thus be tolerated on grounds of political expediency, then by way of contrast, the moderating influence of collectivist economic ideologies is weak, or even non-existent, in the 1985 *White Paper*.

For the past fifty years, the liberal market philosophy has been opposed by liberal collectivists who argue that unregulated markets produce a degree economic inequality and social division which is unacceptable in a political democracy; they urge that the appropriate response is a positive policy of intervention to remedy the consequences of the market. In the 1985 *White Paper*, liberal collectivism survives vestigially in the form of an uneasy conscience about the distributional consequences of the 1992 programme; 'by increasing the possibilities for human, material and financial resources to move without obstacle to the areas of greatest economic advantage, existing discrepancies between regions could be exacerbated' (EC, 1985, abridgement, p. 3). As a sop to conscience, the Community's social and regional funds are then invoked: 'full and imaginative use will need to be made of the resources available through Community funds' (ibid.). This concession is much less generous than it sounds. As we argue in our Chapter Three evaluation of EC regional and social policy, the resources of the regional and social funds are quite inadequate to the task of redressing major inequalities. We are also able to show that EC expenditure from these two funds is in any event channelled into approved liberal market objectives – principally infrastructural improvement and youth training – and this is done through a matching grant system which seeks to redirect national government expenditure into the same limited channels.

The history of the EC is that of an unequal struggle between liberal market and liberal collectivist ideologies. The authors of the Treaty of Rome intended to create a liberal market institution because the removal of trade barriers such as tariffs and quotas was a defining feature of the Community. But free trade was not sacrosanct, regardless of the consequences; Article 109 of the Treaty of Rome envisaged the possibility of protectionist measures as a means of dealing with balance of payments crises in unsuccessful member countries. And the Treaty anticipated a positive role for (macro)economic policy; Article 104 of the Treaty of Rome states that 'economic policy should ensure full employment'. But the liberal collectivist articles have never been applied in a way which challenges liberal market principles. For example, in the case of member countries with balance of payments problems, breaches of free trade have been resisted. And when Community aid has been provided to countries in payments difficulties, like Greece in 1985, the Community has always insisted on orthodox deflationary policies (EC, 1988c, p. 149; EC, 1985a). At every point of choice, liberal market principles have been applied. The 1985 *White Paper* consolidates these tactical victories by proposing a strategy from which all traces of liberal collectivism have been effectively expunged.

None the less, the initial avoidance of monetary policy, as well as the circumvention of the CAP issue, clearly signals that the programme is not simply an example of 'liberal market economics in action'. If we then ask 'What is its driving force?' we can only reiterate that the answer is spelt out with total clarity in the conclusion to the *White Paper*: while the internal market programme is important 'it is not the ultimate goal' (EC, 1985, p. 55). The programme for 1992 is the prelude to political unity; it is an economic means to a political end.

This programme is now becoming a reality. The 1985 *White Paper* identified 300 actions necessary to remove NTBs (these were later reduced to 279). By the Spring of 1989 much was already in place; 232 directives had been submitted, of which 119 were awaiting adoption. Less than 50 were still to be drawn up and submitted. At the same time, the pace was slackening because no progress was being made on some of the more difficult issues like fiscal harmonisation (see Kay, 1989), rights of residence, tax checks and health standards affecting the free movement of food. But the political aim of restarting the process of European unification seems to have been triumphantly achieved. By the late 1980s, the political momentum achieved via the 1992 programme allowed the Commission to address the issue of monetary policy, which had been too problematic in the early 1980s. The Delors Committee, which was appointed in 1988, reported in Spring 1989 and proposed a timetable for economic and monetary unification starting from 1 July 1990 (*Financial Times*, 18 April 1989). The nature of this next phase is considered in our final chapter. At this point we now wish to consider the economic consequences of the 1992 programme.

The Christmas tree approach

The *White Paper* of 1985 contains a variety of assertions about the economic benefits of the 1992 programme (e.g. EC, 1985, abridgement, p. 9). But these assertions have no theoretical back-up or empirical content. The Commission initiated a massive research project on 'the costs of non-Europe' in 1986 *after* the removal of NTBs had been decided. This project was an instance of the most modern kind of sponsored, large-scale research; no fewer than 39 firms of consultants were engaged to work under the supervision of academic advisers and teams from the Commission. The Commission published 27 research reports in 16 bulky volumes. The main results, together with some supporting analysis and evidence, are summarised in popular journalistic form in the Cecchini Report, *1992 The European Challenge*, which was published in Spring 1988; at the same time a special issue of the *European Economy* journal presented the same material in a more technical way for a more professional audience of economists (EC, 1988). Seldom in the history of social research have so many been paid so much to produce such negligible results.

The Commission itself was gratified to find that all its researchers concluded that 1992 would bring positive benefits: 'it is unlikely that the intellectual input of so many leading commentators, academics, officials and independent experts would be unanimously pointing in the wrong direction' (Cecchini, 1988, p. 16). In the circumstances, this unanimity is less reassuring than is claimed. Since the consultants were all directed to investigate 'the costs of non-Europe' in various fields, it would have been surprising if any team had concluded there were no benefits from removing NTBs. The nudge given by the overall terms of reference would in any event have chimed in well with the presumptions of orthodox economic discourse, which, as we argued in the last chapter, has a strong *a priori* bias in favour of free trade and market integration. The economists could happily play a priestly role, just like bishops blessing battleships. It is, then, neither surprising nor particularly impressive that the findings point in the same general direction. What is more contentious is the scale, certainty and pace at which Europe will be propelled down this road. Given the design of the project, it was reasonably predictable that the research teams would each conclude that the 1992 programme was a good thing. The only question was how much of a good thing.

The introductory material and the summary of results in the Cecchini Report claim that the 1992 programme will bring large benefits. In a foreword to the Report, Lord Cockfield, the chief architect of the 1992 strategy, was quietly exultant: 'now we have the hard evidence, the confirmation of what those who are engaged in building Europe have always known' (Cecchini, 1988, p. xiii). According to Cockfield, the removal of NTBs offers 'a prospect of significant inflation-free growth and millions of new jobs'. The overall summary of the gains which will flow from the removal of NTBs is that, 'there would be a medium-term increase in GDP of 7 per cent, unaccompanied by inflation, and the creation of 5 million new jobs' (Cecchini, 1988, p. 102). These very large gains are 'best-case' estimates at the top end of the range of possibilities; the summary section of Cecchini claims were precisely that the re-moval of NTBs can add 4–7 per cent to the Community's GDP (Cecchini, 1988, p. xvii). But, even if the outcome is not best-case, the gains in consumer welfare are such, the Commission maintains, that market integration is not only a good option, it is the only option. Lord Cockfield claims 'no other approach to the challenge of Europe's economic future could possibly offer so much' (Cecchini, 1988, p. xiv).

Those who carefully read the main body of the Cecchini Report and then refer back to the 16 research volumes will come to rather different conclusions. In this respect the EC research project is like the old *London Evening Standard* where there was always a disjuncture between the dramatic promise of the headline on the placard and the boring story on page 5 of the paper. The only difference is that Cecchini's headline claims can only be evaluated if we piece together a variety of different arguments and bits of evidence.

The Commission's researchers point out that the benefits will appear over a period of time. Broadly this translates into a three-stage calculation of the gains from market integration:

Stage 1: Direct micro-economic benefits which arise as consumers are able to buy cheaper products and producers can sell on a wider market after removal of non-tariff barriers.

Stage 2: Indirect micro-economic benefits which arise from 'supply side shock' as increased competition and restructuring to exploit the economies of scale drives down costs and prices.

Stage 3: Macro-economic benefits which arise as supply side effects loosen the constraints on public policy and allow expansionary fiscal policy which amplifies the micro-economic benefits.

The three stages are steps in an argument about different kinds of benefits, and to some extent, they are also time periods which follow one after another as the different benefits materialise. The crucial point is that the headline claims in Cecchini are obtained by adding together the gains made at Stages 1, 2 and 3. That is important because, as we shall demonstrate, the positive gains in producer welfare and the larger gains in consumer welfare only arise in Stages 2 and 3 at the end of a long and hypothetical chain of events with many 'ifs' and 'maybes' about connection and causality.

In an orthodox economic framework, the Stage One benefits are most certain and least problematic. Stage One presents an orthodox

Table 2.3 EC projection of Stage 1 direct micro-economic benefits from removing non-tariff barriers

		billion ECU	% GDP
(A)	gains from removal of barriers affecting intra-European trade (viz. customers formalities and frontier delays)	8–9	0.2–0.3
(B)	gains from removal of barriers to production (viz. protected public procurement, divergent national standards, regulatory diversity)	57–71	2.0–2.4
(C)	total gains from removing barriers (A+B)		
	(i) for 7 member countries at 1985 prices	65–80	2.2–2.7
	(ii) for EC 12 at 1985 prices	74–91	2.2–2.7
	(iii) for EC 12 at 1988 prices	101–125	2.2–2.7

Source: Cecchini, 1988, p. 84.

comparative static micro-economic analysis of the benefits which consumers obtain through buying more cheaply and producers obtain through selling more widely. The procedure is to measure the direct costs arising from non-tariff barriers. These include: the costs involved in customs checks together with the delays and paperwork associated with intra-EC border stoppages; the higher costs to governments and taxpayers which arise from the effective exclusion of intra-EC bidding for the large body of goods and services bought by the public sector; and the costs imposed on firms by the need to meet the demands of varying national regulations and standards. The removal of these cost-raising obstacles should realise once-and-for-all savings. As usual in economics, the argument about results depends on fierce assumptions about the process of change: first, it is assumed that competitive pressures are strong enough to ensure that any efficiency gains are passed on to the consumer, and second, it is assumed that any resources (especially capital and labour) which are displaced through the removal of NTBs will be rapidly re-employed elsewhere.

The main results are presented in Table 2.3. The original study (EC, 1988d, vol. 3) was mainly based on 1985 information for

seven member states (West Germany, France, Italy, UK, Netherlands, Belgium and Luxemburg): the aggregate gains have been
grossed up to provide an equivalent figure for the current 12
members.

There are good reasons to believe that the Commission's researchers have exaggerated the Stage One savings. The researchers
were not asked to make realistic estimates about the effects of the
partial removal of barriers. Thus, the consultants who worked on
frontier controls were asked to assume that all customs checks
would be removed. As they made clear:

> Our remit was to establish the total costs of controls and procedures
> administered by customs on the assumption that they are *all* avoid-
> able. To the extent that any controls remain after 1992 the actual cost
> saving will be lower than those estimated . . . but it was not our task
> to analyse this (largely political) issue. (EC, 1988d, vol. 3, p. 21)

The same kind of exaggeration arises in other areas, where,
although NTBs are removed, consumers will continue to prefer
local products; the cultural preferences of private consumers and
the chauvinist attitudes of national governments will not be transformed by 1992. For these reasons it cannot be assumed that the
benefits from opening up public procurement and reducing diver-
gent national standards are certain or immediate; the policing of
public procurement decisions will be particularly difficult when so
many goods are bought on grounds other than price.

In areas where barriers are removed and consumers buy mass-
produced products on the basis of price, the Commission's researchers again exaggerate by making arbitrary and optimistic
assumptions about the extent of price convergence. For example, in
the case of financial services it was generally assumed that the price
of each service would fall to the level of the average of the cheapest
four countries. This ignores the obvious point that there are good
real-world causes for the divergences in price of similar financial
services in different countries; and these real-world causes will
persist long after the NTBs are abolished. For example, as long as
French road deaths are twice as high as in Britain, motor insurance
will remain much more expensive in France than in Britain (*Auto-
car*, 19 April 1989). Even within culturally homogeneous national
economies, the principle of price convergence does not operate
strongly. The Commission's own research, for example, shows
that there are large and unexplained differences in the price of

electronic consumer goods within the German national economy; the German inter-city price difference on consumer electronics is 53 per cent of the EC international difference (Cecchini, 1988, p. 79; EC, 1988, p. 122).

The conclusion must be that the Commission's Stage One estimates of direct gains are greatly exaggerated. And the Commission's problem is that, even with the benefit of exaggeration, the Stage One gains are very small. Stage One yields a once-and-for-all benefit equal to 2.2–2.7 per cent of GDP or six months growth in a good year. The welfare gain is 101–125 billion ECU, or £68–84 billion sterling at 1986 exchange rates. That looks worthwhile mainly because it is expressed as a global total without any attempt to divide it up between 12 national governments, 320 million consumers and several million firms. If we simplify matters and assume that all the direct gain is expressed in the form of increased consumer surplus, then the once-and-for-all per capita gain is just £198–245. If the aim was solely to increase consumer welfare, much larger gains could be obtained through reform of the Common Agricultural Policy, which, as the National Consumer Council's detailed 1988 study suggests, imposes in Britain a cost of £11.50 a week for a family of four.

The Commission tried again to calculate direct benefits, by different methods, but the results were equally disappointing. In an EC survey, businessmen estimated the direct costs of non-tariff barriers at 40 billion ECU, or just 1.4 per cent of GDP (EC, 1988, pp. 171–2), which is well below the Commission's own bloated Stage One estimates. The consultants reported that: 'In our discussions with trade associations and traders, we have found little evidence to suggest that customs formalities represent a major barrier to trade for newcomers. Rather these procedures are seen as an irritation or an inconvenience to be overcome by successful firms' (EC, 1988d, vol. 3, p. 31). When the direct benefits, however calculated, were very small, the Commission took the Christmas tree approach to calculating benefits. As every child knows, Christmas trees are made more attractive by adding extra decorations and presents. So the Commission introduced the notion of indirect micro-benefits at Stage 2 of its calculations; while the direct and indirect Stage 1 and 2 benefits were to be amplified by fiscal expansion to produce Stage 3 benefits. This approach does produce substantially larger bottom-line gains, but these larger gains are very much less certain. The Commission's boosterism about

Table 2.4 EC projection of Stage 2 indirect micro-economic gains from removing non-tariff barriers

		billion ECU	% GDP
(A)	gains from exploiting economies of scale more fully	61	2.1
(B)	gains from intensified competition reducing business inefficiency and monopoly profits	46	1.6
(C)	total indirect gains (A+B)		
	(i) for 7 member countries at 1985 prices	62–107[a]	2.1–3.7
	(ii) for EC 12 at 1985 prices	71–121	2.1–3.7
	(iii) for EC 12 at 1988 prices	97–165	

[a]The difference between high and low estimates is not explained. A footnote to the original table claims 'this alternative estimate for the sum . . . cannot be broken down between the two steps (A and B)'. The low estimate is of course arithmetically what one would expect if (A) benefits materialised and (B) benefits did not. *Source*: Cecchini, 1988, p. 84.

substantial gains in the Cecchini Report and elsewhere depends on a kind of intellectual sleight of hand: the speculative Stage 2 and Stage 3 gains are consistently presented as nearly certain. Against this, we shall argue in the next section that Stage 2 and Stage 3 gains are unlikely to materialise.

Stage 2 indirect micro-economic benefits

If the Stage 2 and 3 gains materialise, then the 1992 programme is worthwhile. But will supply side shock deliver substantial micro-economic benefits? And will they be amplified by expansionary fiscal policy? Before we address these questions, we can make two general points. First, at Stages 2 and 3, the Commission is not so much modelling economic gains as writing scenarios. The question is whether these scenarios are internally consistent and theoretically or empirically plausible. Second, it is the Commission which makes large claims about the gains at Stage 2 and Stage 3. For critics of the Commission, it is only necessary to demonstrate that Europe is unlikely to develop on the lines envisaged in the official scenarios.

Table 2.4 presents the official EC analysis of indirect micro-economic gains arising in the medium term from 'supply side shock' after 1992. On this scenario, the Stage 2 indirect gains are up to 3.7 per cent of GDP, substantially larger than the Stage 1 direct gains.

Much in the EC's Stage 2 scenario is unclear. For example, Stage 2 benefits will be realised in a 'medium term' time period which is never defined; most commentators have assumed that the 'medium term' means within 6 or 7 years of 1992. But the scenario does explicitly depend on two central presuppositions. First, it is assumed that substantial economies of scale do exist and will be captured through restructuring; economies of scale provide more than half the gains in consumer welfare. Only a small proportion of the scale gain is realised in the short run through improved plant loading when the number of plants and firms is unchanged: 80 per cent of the restructuring gains are achieved in the longer run 'involving the disappearance of the smallest or least efficient companies' (Cecchini, 1988, p. 78) and the larger firms taking greater market share. Merger to realise productive advantage is a crucial instrument in this process because 'mergers and takeovers will permit strategies aimed at better exploitation of returns to scale, wider geographic diversification, and greater international division of labour within the European market' (EC, 1988, p. 135). The second crucial assumption in the EC Stage 2 scenario is that increased competition will both reduce existing monopoly profits and ensure that general gains in efficiency are passed on to the customer.

The assumption about economies of scale is the most obviously controversial element in the Stage 2 scenario. It is internally contradictory, because it cannot be reconciled with the Commission's conclusions about Stage 1, and it is inconsistent with the known facts about international plant size and the established relations between plant size and productivity. If the gains from removing the NTBs are small, as the Stage 1 analysis admits, NTBs are relatively low barriers to entrance in most EC markets. In that case, if there are large potential gains from economies of scale, surely they should have been captured long ago; removal of small NTBs can hardly be a necessary condition for the realisation of large scale economies. Furthermore, much of the Commission's argument appears to rest on the premise that European plants are smaller and, for that reason, less efficient than plants in America, where the market is not fragmented. But the evidence does not show that European plants are usually or generally smaller. Consider, for example, Prais's comparison of median plant size by number of employees in Britain, Germany and the United States (Table 2.5).

Table 2.5 Median plant size by number of employees in Britain, Germany and the United States, 1970–3

	All manufacturing	Light industries	Heavy industries
Britain	440	240	820
W. Germany	410	140	1,080
USA	380	210	810

Source: Prais, 1981, p. 27

In manufacturing as a whole, as well as in heavy industries, British and German plants were larger than American plants, although the margin of superiority was not large and German light industry plants were smaller. A balanced verdict would be that, in general, plant size was similar in all the advanced countries. There are, of course, pronounced size differences in some sectors. But these differences do not have simple direct consequences for efficiency. Caves and Krause (1980) find that plant size has no significant influence on the productivity differentials between UK and American industries.

Why then does the Commission believe that economies of scale are enormously powerful? The belief is justified partly by an appeal to economic theory and partly by an appeal to engineering evidence about the variation of cost in relation to output. What economic theory provides is the concept of the firm's long–run average cost (LRAC) curve; this curve is conventionally supposed to slope downwards to the right over a considerable range of output because fixed costs can be spread over an increasing number of units and because firms can, with increasing output, adopt more efficient capital-intensive methods of production. The other source of support is engineering evidence on the hypothetical minimum efficient technical size (METS); as actual plant size is usually well below the technical optimum, it is supposed that cost reductions can be realised through increasing plant size. The Commission, in effect, tries to hang on to the concept of scale economies by appealing to the stylised constructs of economic theory and engineering. Argument about the merits and demerits of these constructs will continue for years; here and now, all we wish to show is that the constructs will not bear the weight which the Commission puts upon them.

In relation to economic theory, the key question is not whether the LRAC curve slopes down to the right, but whose curve is it anyway? The textbook LRAC curve is constructed as part of a simplified analysis of a firm (or plant) which is producing a single, homogeneous good. For Marshall, this was a useful way of conceptualising the late-nineteenth-century Lancashire cotton firm; the relevance of the construct to Toyota or GEC in the late twentieth century is much less clear. When the multi-product, multi-plant firm is now typical (or commonplace) in all advanced economies, a whole series of complications arise which are not covered in the textbook economic analysis: which costs are economised by an increase in scale and how should these be allocated between plants, products and production runs? Multi-plant and multi-product firms have a variety of cost curves which (according to the accounting conventions adopted) slope in different ways. Even more important, the complexity of multi-plant, multi-process production is such that operations management becomes a major potential source of cost reduction and competitive advantage. Operating efficiency is no longer an unproblematic physical response to the financial pressure of product market competition; operating efficiency has become an important independent variable determining cost levels.

In those practical discourses on management which are not burdened with an obsolete model of the firm, the concept of economies of scale has been increasingly marginalised. The business school gurus now talk of the 'economies of scope' or the firm's ability to produce a flexible mix of products at a reasonable cost (Goldhar and Jelinek, 1983). In guides to best-practice production, by engineers like Schonberger (1982) or Hartley (1987), the emphasis is mainly placed on managing production facilities of a given size to realise lower costs through stock reduction, zero defects and preventative maintenance. The practical discourses have taken on board the lessons of Japanese success and Western failure over the past twenty years. As Cusumano (1985) shows, what Toyota realised in the 1950s and 1960s was that a new kind of operational efficiency could compensate for the disadvantage of smaller plants and shorter production runs, while Western firms who believed in giantism found that increases in size did not necessarily bring benefits in scale. We have elsewhere (Williams et al., 1986) discussed the case of British Steel, which in the 1970s invested huge sums in large-scale BOS steel production at coastal sites. The company believed that bulk steel production must be cheaper because there are simple physical laws about the relation between volume of charge and the surface area of steel converters. In practice, huge losses were incurred, partly because the company could not sell its product and partly because operating efficiency was low when the company had failed to invest in upstream delivery and downstream finishing processes.

The engineering evidence, which the Commission cites in support of scale economies, goes back to an earlier era, before academics were chastened by Japanese success and disillusioned by Western failure. The classic academic studies of scale relate to just three economies (the US, the UK and West Germany) and are based on evidence drawn from the 1960s. Attempts to calculate the minimum efficient technical size of plants (and production runs) figured prominently in this literature. METS was not calculated by comparing the achieved performance of actual plants and lines with different capacities. As in the Commission's more recent work on METS, the METS was determined by asking managers, engineers, accountants and economists for estimates of the hypothetical 'costs of operating at a different scale of production where full adaptation to the scale of production is allowed for' (EC, 1988d, vol. 2 by Pratten, p. 10). The problem with this procedure is that it abstracts from the problem of operating efficiency. There is no possibility that a larger plant could deliver less than its rated capacity, because it is assumed that the plant runs at full capacity, that all processes and lines are fully balanced and that management is capable of operating sophisticated equipment without excessive down time; this last assumption requires in turn the assumption that the equipment is prudently maintained and has no mechanical or electronic design deficiencies. For these reasons, only a brave man would put much faith in the engineering evidence.

If these obstacles were rather lost sight of in the final presentations, they feature prominently in Pratten's careful research report, which reworks and updates the evidence on economies of scale. Pratten's 'survey of the economies of scale' (EC, 1988d, vol. 2) is a cautious piece of work which warns that 'estimates of the economies of scale are elusive' and 'many of the estimates which are available are hedged around with qualifications' (ibid., p. 161). For what they are worth, Pratten's reworked calculations show that the 'long run average cost curve' in European industry slopes down very gently to the right,

- on products and production runs: a doubling of the present EC average run would reduce unit costs by 6 per cent (ibid., p. 83)
- on plant size: if the plant size was half the minimum efficient technical size, unit costs would rise by less than 10 per cent for 70 per cent of the plants and by less than 5 per cent for 40 per cent of a sample of 45 plants across a range of businesses (ibid., p. 94)
- on size of firms: at half the METS, the increase in unit costs would average 9 per cent for six trades (ibid., p. 95).

The implication of these results is that the so-called economies of scale cannot sustain the weight placed upon them by the Commission. Over the range of output increase which is likely after 1992, the decline in costs is likely to be modest or negligible; after all, a 'doubling of the present average run of output in European manufacturing' would take us well beyond most people's conception of what is likely after 1992.

We would not wish to invert the myth of scale and to endorse the newly fashionable notion of 'flexible specialisation', whose confusions and ambiguities we have criticised elsewhere (Williams et al., 1987). In businesses like cars and telecomms, where product-specific development costs are high, long production runs are a source of advantage. And in other businesses, the cost and inflexibility of production equipment is a constraint on very small-scale production. But increases in plant size and line capacity are not the only source of cost reduction, nor are they an infallibly reliable source; a large increase in size is necessary before there is any possibility of significant cost reductions. The balance of argument and evidence suggests that significant cost reductions could only be realised if there were a massive general increase in European product runs and plant size and if management were at the same time able to maintain (or improve) operating efficiency. If the benefits are to go to consumers, then one must add (as the Commission does) the supplementary assumption that competition is maintained so that the benefits of scale are not retained as monopoly profits by big business.

The end result is a post-1992 scenario which is constructed by piling up one conjecture upon another. And the accumulation of 'ifs' does not add up to a possible future when the conjectures about productive restructuring cannot be reconciled with the supplementary assumption about competition. On the one hand the

Commission envisages a process of wholesale productive restructuring which is likely to result in Community markets being dominated by a small number of large firms; on the other hand, the Commission assumes that competition in product markets will be maintained. The Commission's attempts to cover the internal contradictions of the Stage 2 scenario are unconvincing. On the Commission's evidence, in many sectors METS could be realised through larger plants without reducing the number of plants to a handful. The Pratten survey claims that, over sectors covering 63 per cent of European manufacturing output, plants which realised METS would account for 5 per cent or less of total European manufacturing output. The implication is that this is quite enough to maintain competition. But arguments about the technically necessary number of plants cannot be used to justify conclusions about product market competition. The key question is how many of the large number of plants will be owned by a small number of multi-plant firms. This question is not posed or answered in the Commission's research.

Merger does figure prominently as an instrument of restructuring in the Commission's Stage 2 scenario. But that only introduces further uncertainty about outcomes. If merger is allowed, increasing concentration of output is guaranteed, but it is doubtful whether merger will always or usually deliver increasing productive efficiency. As the Commission itself recognises, there are good mergers and bad mergers: good mergers improve productive efficiency by rationalising capacity, while bad mergers are defensively motivated by financial calculations:

> in view of the frequent failure of horizontal mergers, and the even more frequent failure of attempts at conglomerate diversification we should mistrust amalgamations based exclusively on financial or personal links which do not lead to any genuine integration reflected in an overall strategy. Some mergers ultimately produce groups with no internal coherence and can represent a desperate attempt at survival on the part of ailing companies unable to make any new investment. (EC, 1988, p. 136)

Our argument about these issues is developed in Chapter Four on mergers and joint ventures, which shows that the Commission does not have a coherent policy for preventing bad mergers. As an act of faith, the Commission hopes that the unregulated market will produce productive efficiency through good merger. In micro-economic terms, the market integration of 1992 is not a case of the provision of beneficial supply side shock but an exercise in opening Pandora's box.

What about the workers?

The evil of unemployment figures prominently in the rhetoric of the 1985 *White Paper*: 'What is the central issue, the most harrowing problem that faces us? – unemployment' (EC, 1985, abridgement, p. 8). While the Cecchini Report identifies employment gain as a 'most important' benefit of the 1992 programme: 'perhaps most important of all, is the medium term impact of market integration on employment . . . the European home market of the 1990s raises the prospect, for the first time since the early 1970s, of very substantial job creation' (Cecchini, 1988, p. xix). Readers who have followed our exposition of Stage 1 and 2 micro-economic gains will be puzzled as to where the employment gains will come from and how the benefits of 1992 are to be distributed to workers. At Stage 1 and 2, gains in GDP arise from the removal of the NTBs, and as these cost-raising obstacles to trade are removed, the gains are divided between consumers and firms in the form of increased consumer surplus and profits. Unemployed workers do not figure as beneficiaries in the Stage 1 and 2 scenarios. Indeed, they cannot figure as beneficiaries, because their existence is only grudgingly admitted in orthodox micro-economics, which attributes persistent unemployment to labour market rigidities introduced by the existence of trade unions and the payment of unemployment benefit which prevent the labour market from clearing. Strictly, from this point of view, there can be no connection between 1992 and unemployment, because the level of unemployment is determined by other variables in the micro-economic framework.

At Stages 1 and 2 of the 1992 drama, the workers have just a walk-off part. The Commission repeatedly insists that 1992 means cost reductions; it occasionally concedes that these cost reductions are largely obtained through job loss. This is transparently so with the direct economic gains made at Stage 1. For example, much of the small direct gain from removing frontier controls is obtained by sacking customs officers; some 45,000 customs officers in six Community countries may be affected (EC, 1988d, vol. 1, p. 35). At Stage 2, labour's sacrificial role is less obvious. This is because the Commission's researchers generally avoid discussion of the sources of the indirect gains which they predict. In sixteen volumes of research study, the crucial issue of the precise sources of cost saving is only confronted once – in the EC study of the car industry. The car industry is characterised as a suitable case for restructuring where considerable savings can be made by reducing the number of vehicle platforms used by European manufacturers. To a considerable extent, what is saved, at every stage from R and D to final assembly, turns out to be labour. For example, over one-half of the reduction in direct costs is attributable to labour saving (EC, 1988d, vol. 11, p. 386).

If the European workers' role is to lay down their jobs for the greater prosperity of firms and consumers, the EC argues they shall have their reward in the (medium-term) hereafter. It is impossible to find job gains at Stage 1: as Cecchini admits, 'job losses in customs related areas and their knock on effects might even lead to a slightly negative impact in the short term' (Cecchini, 1988, p. 93). But at Stage 2 the official line is that, in many sectors, a small initial job loss will be followed by a larger medium term job gain as the dynamic benefits come through. This, for example, is the Commission's argument about the effects of removing frontier controls:

> if [job losses] . . . all occur over a short time, [they] could even bring about a relative fall in GDP. Once the initial static effect has passed, however, the favourable dynamic effect of external trade will persist; for the Community as a whole, 200,000 jobs could well be created . . . Even though its effect may seem tiny and even microscopic compared with the level of unemployment in the Community, the abolition of frontier controls remains psychologically and strategically essential. (EC, 1988, p. 159)

For the Commission, the issue of employment is sufficiently important to justify macro-economic simulation of the Stage 2 medium-term job gains. The Commission's procedure in this exercise is to assume neutral fiscal policy and simulate the macro-effects of supply side shock. If all the dynamic benefits at Stage 2 are taken into account, the overall medium-term gain is between 1.3 and 2.3 million jobs, which translates into a middle-range estimate of 1.8 million jobs (Cecchini, 1988, p. 98). This projection should be treated with some caution. To begin with, it is a medium-term benefit which is captured after 6 or 7 years; none of the official macro-simulations shows sustained employment growth in the first two-and-a-half years after the removal of NTBs. The projection also depends on Stage 2 processes occurring in the form that the EC predicts; nearly half the 1.8 million jobs gain is attributed to 'supply side effects'. If these effects do not occur, then the job gain will be much more modest. As we have already argued, Stages 1 and 2 involve a long chain of events and processes, many of which are improbable.

Even if Stage 2 job gains do materialise, the gap between short-term job loss and medium-term gain is such that displaced workers will presumably have to wait some time before they are re-employed. In passing, the *European Economy* article raises the crucial issue of 'whether the "equilibrium" postulate, that all resources released in rationalisation would be re-employed, is realistic' (EC, 1988, p. 155). But after briefly registering the fact that the world is not like economic theory, the lid of the theoretical box is quickly nailed down again with the dismissive assertion that 'undoubtedly, it is only a matter of time before such resources are effectively re-employed' (ibid., p. 156). The complication of waiting time can be ignored, but even then the Commission cannot disguise the fact that the Stage 2 job gain is not large enough to make a real difference to European unemployment rates. As the Commission itself observes, a gain of 1.3 to 2.3 million jobs in the Community 'would not be sufficient to bring about any significant reduction in the current unemployment figure, since the unemployment rate would fall by only 1 or 2 percentage points in the medium term' (ibid., p. 162). On the most optimistic assumptions, the medium-term Stage 2 job gains are too small to be significant.

At this point, the Commission introduces a Stage 3 calculation of additional macro-economic benefits which can be realised because macro-economic strategy will be used to magnify the supply side effects (EC, 1988, p. 151). It is assumed that the supply side effects will ease the constraints on reflation by generally reducing inflation and improving the trade deficits of the weaker countries at the same time as budget deficits are lowered. The reduced budget deficits will occur because 1992 will reduce the cost of government; unnecessary public service jobs in border control will be eliminated, and with the opening of public procurement and liberalisation of financial services, the public sector will be able to borrow and buy from the cheapest supplier. On the revenue side, the increased activity following the removal of non-tariff barriers will lead to extra income for government.

The results of the EC's Stage 3 simulation of macro-economic

69

Table 2.6 EC projection of Stage 3 macro-economic benefits from removing non-tariff barriers

	GDP (%)	Consumer prices (%)	Employ. (mill.)	Public budget balance (in % point of GDP)	External balance (in % point of GDP)
Neutral fiscal policy	4.5	−6.1	1.8	2.2	1.0
Reflationary fiscal policy					
Scenario 1	7.5	−4.5	5.7	0	−0.5
Scenario 2	6.5	−4.9	4.4	0.7	−0.2
Scenario 3	7.0	−4.5	5.0	0.4	−0.2

Source: Cecchini, 1988, p. 101.

benefits are presented in Table 2.6. Using the EC and OECD models of the European Economy, the Commission modelled three different levels of fiscal reflation and compared the results with a policy of fiscal neutrality. In the first scenario, all the benefits of market integration are applied to fiscal reflation; in the second, more modest reflation is carried to the point where there is no deterioration in the Community's external balance; the third scenario is simply a split-the-difference compromise between scenarios 1 and 2.

When fiscal reflation is used to amplify benefits, there is a usefully large gain in GDP from 6.5 to 7.5 per cent, but it is not possible to have something for nothing. All the reflationary scenarios significantly check the fall in consumer prices which occurs with neutral fiscal policy. And the most expansionist scenario, 3, is judged to be 'unrealistic' because it involves 'massive deterioration in the EC's external position' (Cecchini, 1988, p. 101). The Commission's preferred option is the compromise scenario 2 which yields a GDP gain of 6.5 per cent. From the Commission's point of view, the really worthwhile Stage 3 gain is that all the reflationary scenarios show substantial employment gains of 4.4 to 5.7 million. That is what licenses the official EC claim that 1992 will bring 5 million new jobs.

This possible gain of 5 million jobs needs to be set in context. The starting point here has to be the number currently out of work.

The 1988 average of the number unemployed in the EC 12 was 15.9 million: the creation of 5 million new jobs would only reduce the number of the unemployed to the still high unemployment level of 1981. In this respect, fiscal reflation would not close the job creation gap with the United States: US unemployment had already by 1986 fallen to its 1981 level. If 1992 job creation is set in the context of current European unemployment, it is difficult to accept the notion that employment is a 'crucial' indicator of the plan and the central motivation of the planners. It is more a case of *timeo Delors et dona ferentes*. Even with the added ingredient of fiscal reflation, the 1992 programme is a policy for tolerating a permanent high level of unemployment. Demographic trends and the coming cyclical downturn promise to have more effect on unemployment in Europe than does a 1992 in which the only really 'crucial' factor seems to be the unfettered market.

Nevertheless, it would be politically unbalanced to reject policies which would ameliorate the problem of unemployment because they did not solve the problem; a gain of 5 million new jobs is definitely worth having. The real difficulty is that it is very unlikely that 1992 will deliver job gains on the scale which the Commission envisages at Stage 3. There are theoretical and methodological problems about the Commission's simulations at Stage 3, and there are also practical problems about whether national governments will take up reflationary policies. Our argument below is that Stage 3 reflation is a theoretically inadmissible conjecture and a practically unlikely outcome.

With Stage 3, we reach the outer limit of the Commission's conjecture where the gains through macro-amplification are dependent on the prior realisation of micro-gains. If 1.8 million jobs do not materialise at Stage 2 in the medium term, then the macro-gains, after reflation, will be much smaller than 5 million jobs. The procedure of adding or multiplying micro- and macro-gains is, in any case, methodologically inadmissible. The micro- and macro-gains are to some extent theoretically incommensurable; the micro-gains depend on classical assumptions about market clearing, whereas all macro-economic models incorporate quite different assumptions about market stickiness. It is also arguable that the Stage 3 scenario rests on a slide between theory and reality which introduces the objectionable assumption that sequence and causality in the real world mimics the order of presentation in discourse. In the Commission's theoretical argument, Stages 1, 2 and

3 each produce discrete identifiable gains which are realised in sequence; as Stage 2 gains are coming through to ease budgetary constraints, national governments choose reflationary expansion. But real-world choice is more complex when a variety of forces will be acting simultaneously to increase and reduce budgetary constraints; cyclical downturn, for example, is likely to be a major independent influence in the early 1990s. There will never be a real-world moment at which national governments realise that, thanks to 1992, their budgetary position is better than it would otherwise have been and that a reflationary response is therefore appropriate.

Whatever the theoretical niceties, it is of course true that, if national governments do choose co-ordinated reflation in the early 1990s, the level of employment in Europe will be higher than it would otherwise be. If the 1992 programme itself delivered no real economic benefits but created a climate of opinion which favoured co-ordinated reflation, that would be a major gain. But however the 1992 programme is hyped, substantial positive policy changes are unlikely. Co-ordinated reflation depends on definite political preconditions, and it is hard to see how these conditions can be met in the EC of the early 1990s.

At no stage does the Commission confront the political difficulties which stand in the way of reflation. There is no possibility of the weaker countries going it alone when they are all balance of payments constrained. Reflation in one country will simply lead to a replay of the ill-fated Mitterrand experiment in France in the early 1980s. Reflation will have to be achieved through co-ordinated activity by the governments of the 12 member states (or a sufficient weight of them). The key political precondition is a progressive consensus about the desirability of reflation amongst 3 or 4 of the leading European countries (including Germany). Practically, that would require the simultaneous election of centre or centre-left governments committed to fiscal expansion in the leading member states. At the time of writing (Spring 1989), Germany's restrictive policies remain a roadblock. Even if the Christian Democrats lose power, these policies may not change dramatically. As we argued in Chapter One, German industrial success has been partly built on domestic restraint which curbs prices and encourages export production; why should the Germans change a winning formula? Furthermore, if substantial co-ordinated reflation is planned, it will be necessary to create supra-national institutions and mechanisms of co-ordination to manage reflationary injections and probably to recycle surpluses and deficits. But the creation of a Euro-Treasury is not on anybody's agenda. Without institutions which could manage and enforce reflation, a recalcitrant country which chose not to reflate could simply go its own way. As the other EC countries reflate, a recalcitrant country is likely to benefit from an improved trade balance and would be under no market pressure to conform.

The fundamental point is that the prerogatives of national government over fiscal policy are such that it is not yet within the Commission's power to order or to require co-ordinated reflation. And after the publication of the Delors Committee Report, what the Commission is now doing to reduce the prerogative of national governments over monetary policy will eventually bestow such power but under an institutional arrangement which will make co-ordinated reflation less likely, not more likely.

Because monetary policy was an issue deliberately avoided in the 1985 *White Paper*, the Cecchini Report discussed only fiscal reflation. But fiscal reflation has to be supported by expansionary monetary policy. If monetary policy is restrictive, then fiscal expansion can be countervailed and frustrated. This is what happened at a national level inside Germany after 1973; the federal government embarked on fiscal expansionism which was counter-weighted by the decisions of the politically independent Bundesbank to maintain restrictive monetary policies. Worse is likely to happen in the Europe of the mid-1990s. The Delors Committee now proposes to create a new supra-national European central bank (ESCB); the political independence of this institution is to be guaranteed so that the Commission will never be able to instruct the ESCB to abandon the kind of sound (restrictive) monetary policies which bankers generally favour. Worse still, it is proposed that, from 1 July 1990, all twelve currencies will be brought into the EMS, and realignment of exchange rates will increasingly become an adjustment mechanism of the last resort to be used 'in exceptional circumstances'. If the weaker countries are prevented from devaluing, the implication is that they must adjust to payments deficits by adopting restrictive domestic monetary and fiscal policies. By the mid-1990s, what the Delors Committee terms 'compatibility of fiscal policies' could mean that the ESCB would enforce co-ordinated deflation in the peripheral countries.

As Beckett's characters waited for Godot, who did not turn up in

73

the third act, so we must wait for co-ordinated reflation, which is not likely to appear in the third stage. Meanwhile, we can try to avoid the kind of inconsequential chatter which passes the time in Beckett's plays. The important thing is to concentrate on the real European issues, which have not been identified or engaged in the 1992 debate. The Cecchini Report, for example, ignores the crucial issue of the distribution of gains from trade between different European countries; all the official calculations show the benefits of 1992 for all the citizens, companies and governments in Europe. As Chapter One argued, the real issue is how trade operates in a primary way to benefit Germany and disadvantage the rest. This chapter shows that, although 1992 will not have large-scale economic effects, the new integrationist monetary policies are likely to reinforce the disadvantage of the periphery. The next chapter will show that EC regional and social policy cannot compensate the disadvantaged.

Independent economists like Geroski (1988) and Neuberger (1989) have evaluated 1992 in studies which, whilst they cannot quite break away from the terms of the economists' debate, are nevertheless sharply critical of the official economic justification of 1992. Neuberger, for example, argues that 'the Cecchini studies cannot bear the weight put upon them' (Neuberger, 1989, p. 1), and that the whole research contains so many errors and inconsistencies that it is 'little short of a disgrace to the economics profession' (ibid., p. 15). The implication is that the 1992 programme was a kind of political stunt which led to an economic confidence trick. As Geroski writes, 'the 1992 programme has been the subject of an extraordinary amount of PR hype, most of which has involved exaggerating the benefits of the 1992 policies and neglecting their costs' (Geroski, 1988, p. 22). This economists' verdict is at one level true enough, while at another, more fundamental level, it is somewhat beside the point. As we emphasised at the beginning of this chapter, the Commission's primary objectives were always political. If the 1992 programme has restarted European unification, then from the Commission's point of view, 1992 is not a stunt but a brilliant political success. And if the economic benefits turn out to be negligible, that should only surprise the more blinkered type of liberal market economist. The results of economic reform will always be negligible, if policy makers privilege and attack imaginary problems about barriers and rigidities whose priority is discursively predetermined inside the theoretical framework. The removal of NTBs was never going to be significant enough to revitalise the European economy, but it has already reactivated the political momentum for European unity.

Chapter 3
Regional Policy or
Liberal Market Tutelage

In Chapter One we reviewed the results of three decades of free trade in the European Community and showed that in such a free-trade area there has been little incentive for producers in the dominant economy, Germany, to locate production in other member states. The absence of trade barriers has meant that the successful have stayed at home and exported; to this extent, the creation of the EC tended to exacerbate inequalities in living standards between nations and regions in the Community. If, then, Community policy on trade barriers affects relative living standards, it is logical for the Community to respond to such problems by developing a regional policy: the European Regional Development Fund was set up in 1975, and its object is to use funds from the Community budget to correct the 'principal regional imbalances within the Community' (Council Regulation 1787/84).

The internal market programme is designed to further free trade by removing the various non-tariff barriers within its scope. Naturally, this raises the question as to whether this new instalment of 'freer trade' will aggravate regional and national inequalities in living standards. Much of the official literature on 1992 provides a sanguine answer to this question. Thus, Cecchini argues that, 'recent developments in trade theory and past experience with the removal of intra-EC tariff barriers indicate that redistributive effects in the wake of freer trade need not be excessive' (Cecchini, 1988, p. 105). In line with this bland conclusion, a muted approach to policy in this area is suggested: 'assistance will be needed for the Community's declining regions and labour affected by industrial restructuring'.

However, a quite different approach is taken in an important semi-official report to which we shall return on a number of occasions in this chapter: *Efficiency, Stability and Equity* was the product of a group chaired by Tommaso Padoa-Schioppa, the deputy director of the Banca d'Italia and, previously, a senior Commission official. The report was undertaken at the behest of the Commission, and the brief of the group was to investigate, 'the economic consequences of the decision taken in 1985 to enlarge the Community to include Spain and Portugal and to create a market without internal frontiers by the year 1992' (Padoa-Schioppa, 1987, p. ix). This report's conclusions are much less sanguine than Cecchini's: 'There are serious risks of aggravated regional imbalance in the course of market liberalisation' (ibid., p. 5). Padoa-Schioppa also takes a different view of the lessons of both theoretical analysis and historical experience: 'any easy extrapolation of "invisible hand" ideas in the real world of regional economies in the process of market-opening measures would be unwarranted in the light of economic history and theory' (ibid., p. 10). Correspondingly, the Padoa-Schioppa report envisages a much more extensive role for regional policy: 'In a larger and more differentiated Community, redistributive functions performed through the budget and the lending instruments of the Community should be considerably developed in size and made more effective in their purpose and design' (ibid., p. x).

The problem of regional inequality

Before turning to discuss the character and effects of EC regional policy, it is sensible to begin with a brief overview of the problem to be confronted. Table 3.1 provides some basic evidence on regional inequalities in income level within the EC 12. The figures are for Gross Domestic Product per head in selected regions; they are calculated on a purchasing power parity basis and provide the best available measure of differences in living standards. The table shows that there are large disparities in income level, with per capita income in the EC's wealthiest regions four or five times larger than in the poorest regions. It is equally significant that these inequalities of income have widened in the 1980s. In an earlier period from 1960 to the mid-1970s there was a marked reduction in inequality within the EC 12. Since then, the process of equalisation has halted and, to some extent, gone into reverse. The net result is that the range of variation in per capita GDP in 1985 was at the same level as that prevailing in 1970 (Keeble, Owens and Thompson, 1982; Keeble, Offord and Walker, 1988; EC, 1987a).

The pattern of income inequality provides a kind of relief map of economic development and underdevelopment, progress and decline. It illustrates the lesson of our first chapter about Germany's predominance in manufacturing and trade. Half of the ten wealthiest regions are located in West Germany, the country with one-third of EC manufacturing capacity and a current-account surplus in trade in manufactured goods with all except one of the other member states. Most of the rest are in 'greater Germany', the areas of Holland, Belgium and northern France which are adjacent to Germany. Table 3.1 also shows that the Commission is faced with two distinct types of regional problem; a problem of general underdevelopment in southern Europe and a problem of decline in some long-industrialised regions of northern Europe. As Padoa-Schioppa argues, 'the least favoured regions' are in the underdeveloped South. These regions are

> characterised by a deficient basic infrastructure and low productivity. In most cases they are located at the Community's periphery. Their income per capita is very low (less than 75 per cent of the Community average) and the share of total income from a low productivity agricultural sector is relatively large. (Padoa-Schioppa, 1987, pp. 162–3)

There is a separate problem of 'declining industrial regions' in north Europe which have suffered through the eclipse of traditional industrial activities like mining, steel, textiles and ship-building. As a result of this structural weakness, in these declining industrial regions 'GDP per capita is between 75 and 100 per cent of the Community average and unemployment is above the Community average' (Padoa-Schioppa, 1987, p. 163).

When Europe's inequalities are large, growing and deep-seated, the most obvious question is whether EC regional policy is adequate to a formidable task of redistribution. In this chapter we provide an answer to this question by examining an interconnected series of issues about objects of expenditure, commitment of resources and mechanisms of distribution. An adequate regional policy must, first, identify strategic objects of expenditure where a commitment of resources will generate a reduction in inequality. Resources would then have to be committed to those objects on a

Table 3.1 Gross Domestic Product per capita in the EC (selected regions) in 1985

Rank	Country	Region	GDP, Per Capita (PPP) EC 12=100
1	Greece	Thrakis	43.2
3	Spain	Extremadura	46.6
5	Italy	Calabria	54.4
6	Portugal	Portugal	54.6
11	Spain	Andalusia	58.3
22	Ireland	Ireland	69.5
34	Belgium	Namur	80.9
35	France	Limousin	81.4
37	Holland	Friesland	82.4
49	UK	Northern Ireland	89.7
56	Spain	Madrid	91.1
60	UK	South Yorks	92.1
72	UK	Cleveland	94.6
127	Italy	Piedmont	110.6
138	France	Alsace	118
151	Italy	Valle D'Aosta	137
152	Germany	Oberbayern	142.7
153	Denmark	Hovedstads regionen	142.9
154	Germany	Berlin (West)	144.4
155	Germany	Bremen	148.7
156	Germany	Darmstadt	150.4
157	UK	Greater London	155.1
158	France	Ile de France	159.4
159	Germany	Hamburg	195.5
160	Holland	Groningen	237.4

Source: Padoa-Schioppa, 1987.

scale sufficient to reduce inequality: a viable strategy of redistribution will be compromised if it is inadequately resourced. The question of mechanisms is also important in the case of a supranational regional policy that aids national governments which have different expenditure priorities and revenue sources. As we shall see, general purpose grants which subvent the revenue of national governments will have effects which are different from grants made for specific purposes. The issue of policy mechanisms may seem tedious and technical, but in our view, it is at least as important as the issue of resources. For this reason the mechanisms issue occupies a central place in our analysis of EC regional policy.

Much discussion of EC regional policy avoids serious analysis of the crucial issues about objects of expenditure, resource commitment and policy mechanisms. This failure to analyse the central problems is particularly striking in the case of those on the left of European politics, who expect great things of regional policy. As we argue in Chapter Five, the typical left response to 1992 has been to argue that the existing liberal market programme should be balanced by a new 'social Europe' programme, and an expanded EC regional policy usually figures as a major part of the social Europe programme. It is assumed that regional policy already redistributes to disadvantaged regions and, if expenditure is increased, that the redistribution will effectively redress inequalities. This is largely delusory. Under the EC's regional policy, expenditure is concentrated on two objects, infrastructural improvement and the training of workers. As we shall see, modest sums are currently spent on these objects, and under scrutiny the Commission's plans for increasing this expenditure are unimpressive. Furthermore, the objects of expenditure are such that even an expanded commitment of resources would not secure a reduction in inequalities. More fundamentally, the left completely misrecognises the character of EC regional policy. The priority accorded to infrastructural improvement and training reflects liberal market prejudices against interfering with the market. And the mechanisms of policy are such that a large expansion of EC regional expenditure, as envisaged in Padoa-Schioppa, would offer poorer countries not assistance but liberal market tutelage which would constrain expenditure by national governments on 'social' objects.

Objects of expenditure

The 1985 *White Paper* asserts that, after 1992, 'full and imaginative use will need to be made of the resources available through the structural funds' (EC, 1985, p. 8). The so-called 'structural funds' to which the *White Paper* refers are the European Regional Development Fund (ERDF), the European Social Fund (ESF) and the 'guidance' section of the Agricultural Guidance and Guarantee Fund. All these funds are financed from the European Community Budget, and there is one important mechanism common to all of them. In general, applications for financial support for projects are submitted from individual member states, and if the project application is approved, then a percentage of the cost is met from the fund concerned. The mechanism is such that each fund works by providing specific-purpose grants which cover part of the cost of particular projects or groups of projects rather than the more open general-purpose grants. This mechanism has several important effects; the most direct and obvious effect is that it allows the Commission to determine the objects of expenditure. And this power has been used to concentrate expenditure on infrastructural improvement and vocational training. This can be illustrated from a brief examination of the pattern of expenditure of each of the three funds.

In the case of the ERDF, grant allocations are, broadly speaking, divided between infrastructural investment and industry, service and craft activities. Examples of projects in the former category include road building programmes, attempts to improve telecommunication networks and to develop energy supply systems. Subsidies to set up industrial enterprises come into the latter category (for illustrations from specific countries see Leonard, 1988, p. 110). ERDF spending has been completely dominated by support for infrastructural projects. Over the period 1975–86 commitments (funds allocated) for infrastructural programmes made up 81.6 per cent of the total, industry, services and crafts accounted for just 16.6 per cent (EC, 1988a, Table 22, p. 72).

Expenditures under the ESF have also been concentrated on a particular objective. In this case the privileged area has been vocational training, to which over 80 per cent of funds were committed in 1986. Wage and recruitment subsidies, the other major category of expenditure, play a much less significant role. In recent years, ESF training expenditure has been concentrated almost entirely on training young people; 75 per cent of commitments in 1986 were allocated to training those under the age of 25.

Expenditure on the 'guidance' section of the Agricultural Guidance and Guarantee Fund (AGGF) is part of the expenditure on the Common Agricultural Policy. The overwhelming preponderance of CAP expenditure goes on price support for agricultural commodities, and a much smaller sum is allocated to 'structural policy', which is funded from the 'guidance' section. The role of the fund is to promote one of the objectives of the CAP set out in Article 39 of the Treaty of Rome: the aim is to 'increase agricultural productivity by promoting technical progress and by ensuring the rational development of agricultural production'. To this end the guidance fund has provided finance for improving 'production structures' through projects which involve reparcelling land, irrigation and

Table 3.2 European Social Fund breakdown of commitments by type of programme, 1986

Programme type	Sums committed (million ECU)	Share of total (%)
Vocational training	2,064.4	80.8
Vocational guidance	19.5	0.7
Recruitment subsidies	269.4	10.3
Wage subsidies	73.3	2.9
Other	125.4	4.9
Total	2,553	100

Source: *Fifteenth Report on the Activities of the European Social Fund*, Brussels, European Commission, 1987.

improving the marketing and processing of agricultural commodities. This is the agricultural equivalent of infrastructural investment to benefit industry.

If the objects of expenditure are considered, it is thus clear that the EC aims to raise living standards in the laggard regions by indirectly influencing the location of industry. The presumption is that (re)location decisions can be influenced and the competitiveness of industry in those laggard regions can be improved by investing in infrastructure and training young workers. Put another way, the point is that the EC approach eschews more direct techniques of intervention in location which are used by many national governments. The EC does not, for example, offer financial inducements in the form of investment grants or accelerated depreciation allowances to firms which locate in disadvantaged areas; equally, the EC does not use direct physical controls to block expansion at the centre and force firms to locate in peripheral or disadvantaged regions. The EC's choice of techniques is inspired by liberal market economics. Expenditure on infrastructure and training are acceptable in a liberal market framework because they can be represented as 'enabling the market to work more effectively'; improving physical communications integrates the market, while training enables adaptation to market-induced changes. Clearly, this cannot be said of direct measures which would operate through the erection of non-tariff barriers of the kind which the Commission is ostentatiously removing under the 1992 programme. The Commission operates a strictly kosher regional policy where liberal market economists play the role of the Beth

Din in supervising ingredients and preparation procedures.

All this means that EC regional policy is ideologically sound, but there must be serious doubts as to whether this kind of 'indirect' policy can redress substantial regional income inequalities. There are strong reasons for doubting that infrastructural improvement is the key to developing the underdeveloped regions of southern Europe or that training is the key to reversing industrial decline in northern Europe. Policies of this kind have dominated EC regional policy with no obviously dramatic effects on regional inequalities. No doubt the execution of the indirect policy has been compromised by limited resources; that point is considered in the next section of this chapter. But more fundamentally, the balance of argument and evidence suggests that the indirect policy is inherently ineffectual.

The official EC literature has argued that the infrastructural endowment of the underdeveloped southern regions is inadequate; it is also asserted that the improvement of infrastructure will generate development, growth and rising real incomes on the periphery. This last assertion rests on the assumption that there is a causal link between infrastructural improvement and economic development and growth.

There are many problems with substantiating such a link. In the case of transport and communications, studies have shown a strong statistical *association* between economic development measured by per capita income and development of 'infrastructure' (Fullerton and Gillespie, 1988, pp. 88–90). However, this evidence does not indicate a direction of causality and thus does not show that infrastructural investment will necessarily create economic growth. This is not to deny that there could be circumstances where a causal link did exist and could be activated by infrastructural improvement. Where, for example, there exists a communications bottleneck which prevents successful export of goods or services, infrastructural investment might then allow a region to realise comparative advantage. Some authorities in the peripheral regions believe that their economies will gain in this way from infrastructure improvement; the governor of the Irish central bank claims that Ireland would realise substantial advantages if it had the benefit of an hourly ferry service (*Financial Times*, 12 December 1988). But it has never been demonstrated that the circumstances of the peripheral economies do fit the hypothetical case. Much investment in infrastructural improvement is probably double-edged in its effects. Better communications promote development and raise incomes by facilitating exports from the region or country; at the same time, the better communications can facilitate imports into a region or country, imports which may reduce employment and have adverse distributional effects. In an EC which is dominated by German manufacturing, it would be unwise to ignore the negative effects of improved communications in peripheral regions.

In the declining industrial regions of northern Europe, there is said to be no problem about physical infrastructure, which is 'generally relatively satisfactory' (Padoa-Schioppa, 1987, p. 163). The official EC diagnosis is that these areas will benefit from training because they are 'in need of reconversion and professional educational programmes' (ibid., p. 163). But the success of training measures will be conditioned by the extent to which they relate to employment opportunities. Ideally, training programmes should relieve actual shortages of skilled labour. Equally, given the significance of the trade constraint identified in our first chapter, training should be linked to economic developments which will help ease this constraint.

The key preconditions are not satisfied in the case of the UK, which is the national economy most characterised by 'declining industrial regions'. The major training initiative of the 1980s in the UK was the Youth Training Scheme (YTS), which was designed to give 16 and 17 year olds a combination of on and off the job training. It started as a one-year scheme and was extended to two years in 1985. In both formats the 'on the job' element dominates; off the job training accounted for only twenty weeks even in the two-year programme. Part of the rationale for the YTS was that it would contribute to improving the overall competitiveness of the UK economy. However, this objective sits uneasily with the distribution of YTS places by sector which is given in Table 3.3. What is striking here is the heavy bias of placements towards sectors whose output is not internationally traded. It is true that the programme was designed to generate 'transferable skills', which would be applicable to a range of occupations. But given the limited period of off the job training, this objective must frequently have remained unrealised. The pattern of placement is in any event hardly surprising, in that it simply reflects the pattern of job creation in the UK economy. For example, from September 1984 to September 1988 the number of employees in employment rose by 859,000, but only 220,000 of this increase was accounted for by full-time employment; male full-time employment actually fell by

Table 3.3 Industrial distribution of approved YTS places on Mode A
schemes, 1984–5

Standard Industrial Classification	% of approved places
Agriculture, forestry, fishing	2.9
Energy, water supply	1.4
Minerals, ores, metal	2.1
Engineering	10.2
Other manufacturing	4.8
Construction	9.5
Distribution, hotels, catering	20.4
Transport, communications	3.1
Banking, finance	10.2
Other services	35.3

Source: D. Gray and S. King (1986), *The Youth Training Scheme: the first three years.*

100,000 over this period. Skill training is hardly a high priority in
an economy whose failure in manufacturing trade has meant that
employment is increasingly generated in a service sector which has
a low skill requirement.

Overall, the general conclusion must be that liberal market
principles direct EC regional expenditure onto objects which are
inappropriate in the case of labour training and may be counter-
productive in the case of infrastructural improvement. Worse still,
the internal market programme for 1992 leads to initiatives which
directly countervail the objectives and effects of regional policy.
This is an important but neglected point; the discussion of EC
regional policy is almost never set in the context of other EC
policies. To illustrate the point, we shall consider the case of
telecommunications, where the contradictions between regional
and general policy are acute.

As part of its regional policy of improving infrastructure, the EC
has initiated a major programme for improving and upgrading
telecommunications in the peripheral regions. The STAR (Services
de Telecommunication Avancée dans les Régions) programme was
approved by the Council in October 1986. Over five years STAR
has 780 million ECU committed and is to operate in Greece,
Ireland, the Mezzogiorno, Northern Ireland, Corsica and the
French Overseas Departments. The programme has been introduced at a time when the provision of telecomms services is rapidly
being transformed by electronics. The familiar basic service of
voice telephony is being supplemented with a range of 'advanced

services'; these include telephone transmission of visual images and data, electronic mail and value added network services which allow the accessing of databases (see Vickers and Yarrow, 1988, p. 196). The two objectives of STAR are to provide equipment for the provision of advanced telecommunications services and to promote the use of advanced services in selected peripheral regions. The object of STAR is thus to improve the competitive position of the less favoured regions through the improvement of the communications infrastructure.

However, the Commission's general policy approach to telecommunications has effects which are diametrically opposed. For example, in the edition of *European Economy* devoted to the economics of 1992, the Commission's 1992 policy on telecommunications services is summarised as follows:

> if the telecommunication services sector is to maximise its contribution to the integration and competitiveness of Community industry, it is becoming increasingly apparent that a more appropriate institutional structure is needed. Existing restrictions on network-user and service-producer freedom must be reduced to a minimum and current policy of cross-subsidisation at the expense of long-distance traffic revised. (EC, 1988, p. 99)

The Commission envisages a post-1992 future in which cross-subsidisation will either cease or be severely restricted and services beyond a very basic level will be provided on commercial criteria. This kind of regime must necessarily disadvantage the 'least favoured regions'. Costs of service provision are greater in such areas because lower population density means higher costs; subscriber to operator ratios are lower, and greater length of cable per subscriber is required.

Regional policy pushes in one direction, but 1992 policy pulls in the other. The financial accounts of public telecommunications suppliers show that the choice is sharp and real; for example, in 1983 the Italian national telecommunications enterprise SIP made losses on service provision in the Mezzogiorno equivalent to 46 per cent of operating profits in the rest of Italy (Pye and Lauder, 1987, p. 100). The UK experience of deregulation shows how the choice is likely to be resolved. In the UK the privatisation of British Telecom has resulted in significant changes in relative prices for telecommunications services, with marked increases in the cost of local calls and basic rental charges and falls in the cost of long distance calls. This is exactly the pattern viewed as desirable in the 1992 account since it results from ending the cross-subsidy of local calls. Yet this pattern may well disadvantage enterprises in the poorer regions. Fullerton and Gillespie, for example, report evidence that 'in the UK . . . companies located in the less favoured regions tend to have patterns of communication which are proportionately more local in their orientation than in the case for core-region companies' (Fullerton and Gillespie, 1988, p. 100).

Scale, distribution and 'additionality' of regional expenditure

The argument so far has focused on the issue of the objects of expenditure, which is in many ways the crucial political issue at stake in EC regional policy. A consideration of the other relevant issues only reinforces our pessimism about the effects of regional policy. The distribution of regional expenditure ensures that the poorest countries get the largest share. But the effects of this 'industrial' redistribution are countervailed by the effects of regressive 'agricultural' transfers to richer north European countries under the price support provisions of the CAP. Furthermore, the scale of regional expenditure is very modest, and the mechanisms are such that it is not clear whether the EC provides additional expenditure which sustains projects that would not otherwise have been undertaken.

As we have already seen, the Commission sees the 'structural funds' playing a key role in a redistributive regional policy. However, it is worth bearing in mind that, while, by definition, the object of the ERDF is to reduce regional inequalities in living standards and economic performance, this is less true of the other two funds. In the case of the ERDF its regional role is straightforward. The fund was established in 1975 by a Council regulation; article 3 of that regulation states:

> The purpose of the European Regional Development Fund is to contribute to the correction of the principal regional imbalances within the Community by participating in the development and structural adjustment of regions whose development is lagging behind and in the conversion of declining industrial regions. (Council Regulation 1787/84)

However, for the European Social Fund there is no specific reference to any 'regional' objectives. The aim of the fund is specified in

Article 123 of the Treaty of Rome, where the rationale is described in the following terms:

> In order to improve employment opportunities for workers in the common market and contribute thereby to raising the standard of living, a European Social Fund is hereby established. . . . it shall have the task of rendering the employment of workers easier and of creating their geographical and occupational mobility within the Community.

Similarly, the reference in Article 39 of the Treaty to 'improving productivity and technical progress in agriculture' is a general one with no specific 'regional' focus.

It is, in fact, the case that both the ESF and the 'guidance' section of the AGGF operate with rules which generate biases in favour of the poorer regions. For example, changes in the rules of the ESF in 1983 mean that 44.5 per cent of fund expenditure must be concentrated on seven 'absolute priority' zones. The areas concerned are the whole of Greece, Ireland and Portugal; the Italian Mezzogiorno; Castille-Leon, Castille-La Mancha, Extremadura, Andalusia, Murcia, the Canaries and Galicia in Spain; Northern Ireland; and the French Overseas Departments (Leonard, 1988, p. 115). Biases towards poorer regions also operate in the 'guidance' section, where a larger percentage of the funding of individual projects may be granted if they are in poorer regions and where funds for matching grants are reserved for poorer regions. Nevertheless, the 'bias to the poor' is more pronounced in the case of the regional fund than for the other two funds. This is illustrated in Table 3.4, which shows, for example, that the Community's four poorest countries, with 18.9 per cent of the EC population, obtained 45.6 per cent of ERDF funds, 37.6 per cent of ESF funds and 39.4 per cent of agricultural guidance funds in 1986.

Expenditure from the structural funds is redistributive. What Table 3.4 does not show is that the effects of the structural fund redistribution to poorer southern countries are countervailed by the effects of regressive transfer to richer north European countries which result from the operation of the CAP price support scheme. This is another case where the operations of regional policy need to be set in the context of other EC policies. In a recent article, Ardy (1988) develops a framework for analysing the redistributive effects of the CAP. His article considers the budgetary costs and benefits of Agricultural Guarantee expenditure for different countries, as

Table 3.4 Allocation of European Regional Fund, European Social
Fund and Agricultural Guidance Section expenditure by
country in 1986 and share of EC population by country

Country	share of population (%)	ERDF share (%)	ESF share (%)	Ag-guidance share (%)
Belgium	3.1	0.6	1.2	1.6
Denmark	1.6	0.3	1.9	2.4
Greece	3.0	9.7	5.6	14.3
Spain	11.7	20.1	13.9	8.8
France	17.3	8.1	14.8	21.5
Ireland	1.1	3.9	9.4	8.1
Italy	17.8	25.5	21.7	15.8
Luxemburg	0.1	0.03	0.1	0.2
Holland	4.5	0.9	2.6	2.3
UK	17.5	16.1	16.2	10.6
Portugal	3.1	11.9	8.7	3.4
W. Germany	19.0	2.6	3.9	10.6

*Source: Fifteenth Report on the Activities of the European Social Fund, Brussels, Euro-
pean Commission, 1987; National Consumer Council (1988).*

well as the non-budgetary costs and benefits arising from the
maintenance of EC prices at levels higher than those prevailing on
world markets. Net gain or loss is mainly determined by whether
countries are net exporters or importers of agricultural products.
Because poorer countries are not all substantial net exporters, the
redistributive effects of the CAP are often regressive. As Table 3.5
shows, it is true that in per capita terms, a poor country (Ireland)
obtains the largest net benefit with a gain of 370 ECU per capita.
But three wealthy countries (Denmark, Netherlands and France)
otherwise claim the largest benefits.

A recent investigation of the overall incidence of the EC budget
concluded that whether countries were net contributors or recipi-
ents was 'unrelated to average GDP' (Ardy, 1988, p. 421). The
perverse net redistributive effects arise because large sums are spent
on the CAP and only modest sums are spent on EC regional policy.
Table 3.6 shows that the ERDF and ESF are the dominant structural funds accounting for roughly 85 per cent of structural fund
expenditure in 1988. Even though the ERDF and ESF claim almost
all of regional expenditure, the sum available for regional policy
purposes is modest because the size of the EC budget is limited and
most of the expenditure goes on agricultural price support. The EC

Table 3.5 Per capita CAP benefits, by country, EC 10, 1982–5

Country	ECU	Country	ECU
EC 10	45	Belgium/Lux	21
W. Germany	24	UK	4
France	83	Ireland	370
Italy	8	Denmark	291
Netherlands	155	Greece	45

Source: Ardy (1988), p. 415.

Table 3.6 European Community budget commitments by category of expenditure, 1988

	Commitment (million ECU)	% of total
Agricultural Guarantee	27,500	60.7
'Structural Funds':		
Agricultural Guidance	1,201	2.6
European Regional Development Fund	3,648	8.0
European Social Fund	2,865	6.3
Repayments and administration	5,700	12.6
Other policies	3,213	7.1
Monetary reserve	1,000	2.2

Source: *European Trends* (1989), *Background Supplement 1988–9*.

budget in 1988 accounted for only 1.1 per cent of Community GDP. There are plans to increase the size of the budget, but the target for 1992 is only 1.17 per cent of Community GDP. Table 3.6 also shows that 60 per cent of the EC budget in 1988 was absorbed by the requirements of price support under the agricultural guarantee scheme and that less than 20 per cent was accounted for by the structural funds. However the regional policy money is spent, the sum available is simply inadequate to deal with the centripetal effects of trade and general EC policy and at the same time to redress the existing disadvantages of peripheral and declining industrial regions. Indeed, in some parts of some of the southern countries of the Community the scale of the problem is one of overcoming economic underdevelopment of Third World proportions. Yet given the constraints on the overall size of the EC budget, increased resources for regional policy can only be released

Table 3.7 Quota allocations of shares of ERDF funds by country, 1984

Country	Quota share (%)
Luxemburg	0.2
Denmark	1.1
Belgium	1.4
Holland	1.5
W. Germany	4.7
Ireland	6.9
Greece	11.3
France	11.5
Italy	34.7
UK	26.7

Source: *European Regional Development Fund, Tenth Report*, Brussels, European Commission, 1986.

by a reform of the CAP which reduces the large sums spent on price support. In the next section of this chapter we sceptically consider the Commission's claims that this matter is in hand.

Before we turn to examine CAP reform, we shall consider the issue of 'additionality'. To understand this issue, it is necessary to begin by describing the distributional mechanisms of regional policy. Regional policy was designed to operate in favour of poorer regions, and the Commission has always tried to achieve this objective by devising rules and mechanisms which concentrate resources where they are needed. Until 1985 this distributional objective was effected by assigning each member state a fixed quota share of the overall fund expenditure. Table 3.7 shows the quota allocations in 1984, the last year in which this system operated.

By definition, the point of a Community regional policy would be to increase the resources available and to fund extra suitable projects, over and above those which would have been supported by national governments. However, the quota mechanism operated in a way which makes it doubtful whether additional resources were, in practice, supplied. Governments of member states knew via the quota what they would receive from the regional fund. There was nothing to stop national governments simply deducting their quota allowance from the sums already allocated to regional policy expenditure at a national level. A graphic illustration of this practice is provided by Bruce Millan, who is currently EC Commissioner for Regional Policy. In the late 1970s Millan was a member of the British Labour government as Secretary of State for Scotland; he describes his, and the government's, approach to the ERDF under the quota system in these terms:

> Every quarter we drew up a list of projects or companies due to get national assistance. We knew roughly what the UK as a whole and Scotland would get from the EC each year. So we just picked out as many projects as were needed to make up the UK quota, and sent the list off to Brussels. Back came the EC money, and the Treasury simply lopped that amount off its expenditure. (*Financial Times*, 5 January 1989)

The practice described by Bruce Millan effectively turned the specific purpose grants into general purpose grants which subvented the budget of a member state. Whether quota support grants increased the volume of government expenditure in member states is uncertain; it is at least possible that the main effect of general EC subvention was to reduce public sector deficits in a marginal way. If other national governments behaved as the British government did, EC resources were not being used to fund projects which would otherwise not have started; EC regional grants simply released government resources for expenditure on purposes other than training and infrastructure.

The Commission recognised that the pre-1985 quota system created a variety of problems. It wanted to deal with 'additionality' and also claim a larger political role in the allocation of money. In principle, the Commission should have had the political role of operating regional policy by scrutinising applications for funding and allocating funds on the basis of the merits of each application. In practice, if the member state submitted enough applications in a long list, then the national government would obtain its quota and the scrutinising role of the Commission was nullified. Under the quota system, discretion over the use of resources effectively lay with the government of the member state concerned.

The Commission's first attempt to deal with these perceived difficulties was a reform of the fund in 1979, when a non-quota section was introduced. However, this change did not amount to much, because the non-quota part of the fund accounted for only 5 per cent of expenditure (Croxford et al., 1987, pp. 27–8). A more fundamental reform was introduced in January 1985, when the quotas were replaced by 'indicative ranges'. Each country was now not allocated a fixed share of the fund but rather a minimum and a

Table 3.8 European Regional Development Fund 'Indicative Ranges' applicable in 1986

Country	Lower limit (%)	Upper limit (%)
Belgium	0.61	0.82
Denmark	0.34	0.46
W. Germany	2.55	3.40
Greece	8.36	10.64
Spain	17.97	23.93
France	7.48	9.96
Ireland	3.82	4.61
Italy	21.62	28.79
Luxemburg	0.04	0.06
Holland	0.68	0.91
Portugal	10.66	14.20
UK	14.50	19.31

Source: EC, 1988a.

maximum allocation, which was to apply over a three-year period. Table 3.8 gives the indicative ranges for 1986. The indicative ranges were designed to shift political control to the Commission; as the member states could not now be sure of the size of their allocation, there would be an incentive to increase the number of applications. The Commission would then be able to exercise its scrutinising role and, thus, exert an influence over the shape of regional policy. A further reform animated by the same motives was introduced simultaneously in a new kind of 'Community Programme' where the Commission itself could take the initiative in proposing a programme.

How effective are the 1985 reforms likely to be? To some extent the introduction of 'indicative ranges' has had the sort of effect which the Commission wanted. The number of applications for ERDF assistance increased by 22 per cent between 1984 and 1985, and the volume of funds applied for increased by 88 per cent (Croxford et al., 1987, Table 3, p. 31). The Commission has more projects to choose from, as it had intended. However, the reformed system is not so very different from the old quota system. The indicative ranges set a minimum and maximum share of the fund for each member state, and there is an obvious limit on Commission discretion. Indicative ranges apply over three-year periods, and a member state which is particularly successful in the first two years will find itself bumping up against the maximum allocation in

Table 3.9 European Commission projections for the European Budget, 1988–1992 (million ECU in 1988 prices)

	1988	1989	1990	1991	1992
EAGGF Guarantee	27,500	27,700	28,400	29,000	29,600
Structural Funds	7,790	9,200	10,600	12,100	13,450
Repayments and administration	5,700	4,950	4,500	4,000	3,550
Other policies	3,313	4,035	4,400	4,850	5,200
Monetary Reserve	1,000	1,000	1,000	1,000	1,000
Total	45,303	46,885	48,900	50,950	52,800
Appropriations as %of Community GDP	1.12	1.14	1.15	1.16	1.17

Source: Fifteenth Report on the Activities of the European Social Fund, Brussels, European Commission, 1987; National Consumer Council (1988).

the third year. On the other hand, member states are assured of their minimum entitlement, and with respect to this part of the allocation, there is no reason why the practice described by Bruce Millan should not still operate. This argument is given added force if we bear in mind that 88 per cent of the total allocation is accounted for by minimum allocations; effectively, the 'non-quota' section remains very limited (Croxford et al., 1987, p. 34). The Commission has not solved the problem of additionality.

Reform of regional policy:
(a) enlarging the·structural funds

In the past the structural funds were unable to play a central role in combating regional inequalities, because the resources available were simply too meagre. The Commission now assures us that this matter is in hand and that the resource constraint will be eased. In February 1988 the Commission proposed radical increases in the resources allocated to the structural funds, and these proposals were accepted at the meeting of the European Council in that month. Table 3.9 shows the Commission forecast for the size and distribution of the EC budget for the five years 1988–92. As we can see, the allocation to the structural funds is projected to increase *in real terms* by 70 per cent over the period concerned.

This might seem to be a generous increase. However, the proposed expansion has to be set in the context of the enlargement of the Community. Portugal and Spain both joined the Community in 1986, and these two countries contain many of the poorest regions in the Community (see Table 3.1). A considerable expansion of regional assistance was required simply to meet the new needs of an enlarged Community. Set against this, the fact is that, in the period prior to the reform proposals, the structural funds had been falling behind; between 1985 and 1987 ERDF grants increased by 34 per cent, while over the same period, there was a doubling of the population of Community regions with a GDP per head of less than 75 per cent of the Community average (Lowe, 1988, p. 506). ERDF commitments of expenditure have been consistently biased towards the poorer regions, so the natural consequence of enlargement, with limited resources, was that the very poor gained at the expense of the poor. For example, in 1985 Italy obtained 35.5 per cent of ERDF expenditure and the UK obtained 23.8 per cent; in 1986 the Italian share fell to 25.5 per cent and the UK share to 16.1 per cent. A similar pattern is likely to operate in the future. One of the five main objectives set for Community regional policy in the period to 1992 is 'converting the regions seriously affected by industrial decline'; some 20 per cent of ERDF expenditure is to be directed to such regions. This sounds like good news for the UK, which should be the largest single beneficiary of this policy; the UK contains 19.9 million of the 50 million people living within designated areas of decline. However, if we exclude the EC's allocation to the most deprived area of the UK (Northern Ireland), the UK's ERDF allocation will decline from £355 million in 1988 to £200 million in 1989.

A 70-per-cent increase in the size of the structural funds does not mean similar increases for most of the poorer countries and regions. And the problem of distribution between the poorer and the poorest is intractable because the aggregate sum available for regional purposes will remain modest. After all, the EC expenditure projections show that the EC budget as a whole will rise from 1.12 to just 1.17 per cent of Community GDP. Most of the space for increased regional expenditure is to be created by a projected reform of the CAP which would bring agricultural price-support expenditure under control. Overall, between 1988 and 1992, EC budget expenditure in real terms is projected to rise by 7.5 billion ECU (see Table 3.9). Structural fund expenditure on regional policy is expected to increase, in real terms, by 5.7 billion ECU over the same period. But that increase in regional expenditure can only be funded if increased expenditure on price support from the agricultural guarantee fund is held down to a maximum of 2.1 billion ECU, in real terms, over the five-year period. The target of containing expenditure on agricultural price support is a modest one; the Commission's own projections allow for a real increase of 7.6 per cent in guarantee fund expenditure between 1988 and 1992, and in 1992 the guarantee fund will still account for 56.1 per cent of all EC budget expenditure (Table 3.9). Whether even this target can be met is another matter. In the past the lion's share of the EC budget has been swallowed by the CAP, and other policy areas have been starved of resources. Is it likely that the pattern of history can be reversed and expenditure on the agricultural guidance fund be controlled?

As we saw in Chapter Two, the central feature of the Common Agricultural Policy is the attempt to ensure farmers in the Community a 'fair' standard of living via price support. This involves rigorous protection against imports from third countries and a willingness by intervention authorities to purchase surpluses at an agreed price. The combination of a system with such guarantees, technical progress and slow growth in demand for agricultural products within the Community necessarily generated 'structural' surpluses in agricultural products. In the 1970s the CAP intervention authorities were willing to buy surplus agricultural production on an open-ended basis at a set price which was not affected by the size of the surplus. Attempts at reform in the mid-1980s focused on these two features: the open-ended commitment to purchase and the willingness to purchase at a set price. Different techniques were used to curb expenditure on dairy products and cereals which in 1987 accounted for over 40 per cent of CAP price-support expenditure. In the case of milk, the Commission introduced quotas in 1984. Each member state was allocated a national quota based on deliveries to dairies, and member states then distributed the quota allocation to producers in their own country (National Consumer Council, 1988, pp. 220–1). In the case of cereals a so-called 'guarantee threshold' was applied. Under this system a target level of output is set for the commodity concerned, and if output exceeds the target, the intervention price is reduced. The Council of Ministers agreed to apply a system of guarantee thresholds to cereals when the CAP support prices for 1982/3 were determined. These changes did not involve fundamental alterations in the basic structure of the CAP. There is no change in the system of variable import levies which provides rigorous protection against third country imports. Equally, intervention prices remain operative, although the open-ended commitment to buy output (of sufficient quality) is removed in the case of quotas and the price is cut if the threshold is exceeded in the case of guarantee thresholds.

It is against the background of these half-hearted attempts at reform in the mid-1980s that we should judge the latest reform package, agreed by the European Council in February 1988. This package involves what some commentators see as three new elements: a 'limit' on price-support expenditure; the use of 'automatic stabilisers'; and the introduction of a 'set aside' policy. The limit is a commitment that growth in agricultural guarantee expenditure shall not exceed 74 per cent of the rate of increase in Community GDP. The 'automatic stabilisers' are very much like the old guarantee thresholds; the main difference is that they are supposed to operate in a significantly different way. In the past, price reductions resulting from thresholds being exceeded were never automatic: 'they applied only in the following year, in the form of reductions in the price increases to be decided by the Council of Ministers' (Avery, 1988, p. 524). As a result of political deliberations in the Council of Ministers, many of the proposed price reductions either did not occur or were markedly reduced. In contrast, the new system 'provides for automatic decisions linking reductions in market support to increases in production without further decisions by the Council' (Avery, 1988, p. 526). Finally, the 'set aside' measure is designed to encourage farmers to withdraw arable land from production. Under this system a payment per hectare will be made to farmers taking arable land out of production for a minimum period of five years. At least 20 per cent of the arable land on the farm must be withdrawn, although certain limited agricultural uses are permitted.

This reform package is represented as a new start for the CAP, but there are a number of reasons for scepticism. The new stabilisers are only the old guarantee thresholds with automatic price reductions built in. There is no change in the structure of Community decision making on agricultural policy, where the Council of Ministers remains the supreme body. If the Council of Ministers has regularly suspended the operation of guarantee thresholds before, it is not clear why the Council should not interfere again. Arguably, overt interference is not necessary, because the Council makes its presence felt by ensuring the thresholds are generous and the abatements in price are gentle. This is certainly so in the case of the current guarantee threshold for cereals, where prices will fall by 3 per cent if cereals output exceeds 160 million tonnes. A threshold of 155 million tonnes had originally been proposed by the Commission, but this was revised upwards to 160 million tonnes by the Council. The Commission's proposed threshold was well in excess of current EC levels of demand; the 'domestic use' of cereals in the EC 12 in 1985/6 was just 143.3 million tonnes (EC, 1988b). As far back as 1981, the Commission had proposed a more realistic, but less politically acceptable, target for cereal production in 1988 of 130 million tonnes (National Consumer Council, 1988, p. 217).

Even if automatic stabilisers were to be strictly applied, there is a limit to what they can do, because stabilisers cannot control any of the main categories of expenditure in the price-support policy. Table 3.10 gives a breakdown of agricultural price support expenditure by category in 1986. It shows that roughly a third of expenditure is accounted for by payments to purchase agricultural products; nearly 40 per cent is accounted for by export refunds and 20 per cent by storage costs. Stabilisers cannot control these expenditures, because they impose a price penalty if output exceeds a given level, but they do not put a ceiling on the output of the product concerned. Price-support expenditure is not limited if, for example, there is a good cereals harvest. The intervention authorities are then obliged to buy the surplus output at a slightly reduced price; the increase in volume of output in a good year is likely to be substantially larger than the 3-per-cent price penalty currently imposed. In this situation, surpluses would accumulate, and storage costs would necessarily increase. Surpluses are often disposed of by selling them on world markets at subsidised prices; if excess output is sold in this way, the cost of export refunds will increase.

As Table 3.10 shows, export refunds are the largest single category of expenditure under the CAP. These costs are not controlled by stabilisers, and they are driven by determinants which are exogenous to EC agricultural policy. Surpluses sold on world markets must, necessarily, be sold at prevailing world market prices, and export refunds are required to bridge the gap between support prices and world market prices. If world market prices are lower, then export refunds will be higher. Consequently, increases in overall output of an agricultural commodity on a world scale will depress world prices and push up export refunds. Another key

Table 3.10 Agricultural price policy by category of expenditure, 1986 (expenditure in million ECU)

	Expenditure	% of total
Price support	7,889.5	36.4
Storage	4,375	20.2
Export refund	8,470	39.1
Other	936	4.3

Source: National Consumer Council (1988).

consideration is that export refunds are denominated in ECU, but world market prices for most agricultural commodities are set in dollars. Consequently, a fall in the exchange value of the dollar against other major currencies will lead to a fall against the ECU and thus involve an increase in export refunds. These points were made by the House of Lords Select Committee on European Communities, which concluded pessimistically that,

> Stabilisers cannot be expected to take all the strain of restraining Budget expenditure on the CAP. They cannot control all three of the key determinants of agricultural spending (the level of world market prices for farm commodities, dollar/ECU exchange rates and the weather to be experienced in any particular year) and can control only indirectly levels of agricultural production. (House of Lords, 1988, p. 13)

If the short term prospects for restraining CAP spending are unpromising, will the set aside proposals curb the growth of production in the longer run? For a variety of reasons, this outcome is unlikely. If the price-support system continues (as seems probable) to give incentives for increased output, that will countervail the incentive to take land out of cultivation. This is another instance of contradiction between different EC policies; the Commission's left hand prefers not to know what the right hand is doing. Neither should it be assumed that a crude mechanism like set aside will secure any reduction in output; farmers can 'set aside their least productive land and increase yields elsewhere by using more fertiliser or by more timely operations and better control of pests and diseases' (Consumers in the European Community Group, House of Lords, 1988, p. 36). Finally, set aside will operate with variable effects in different national agricultural frameworks. Set aside is likely to be least effective in France, which is, overwhelmingly, the Community's largest cereal producer; in France, high land taxes impose substantial fixed costs, thus increasing the incentive to spread costs over a large output. With set aside, as with stabilisers, the Commission has failed to introduce mechanisms which are adequate to the purpose of restraining agricultural guarantee expenditure. For this reason it is likely that agricultural spending will continue to crowd out regional policy spending.

Reform of regional policy: (b) a scenario for economic and political tutelage

The Commission's regional policy has always privileged the liberal market objects of infrastructural improvement in the peripheral areas and training in the declining industrial regions. But, as we have argued, the mechanisms of policy are such that liberal market aims have never been realised; under the quota system and its successors specific purpose grants become general purpose subventions of government expenditure in member states. From the Commission's point of view, effective reform means not only increasing the quantum of resources available to the structural funds but also concentrating those resources on appropriate objects of expenditure. Thus EC regional policy reform includes the project of setting up a system of economic and political tutelage. In this section we describe the semi-official plan for tutelage outlined in the Padoa-Schioppa report and explain how this kind of tutelage will limit expenditure by national governments on social objects which are outside the liberal market framework.

An appendix to the Padoa-Schioppa report presents a scenario for development of the least favoured regions on the underdeveloped periphery. 'Deficient basic infrastructure' is assumed to be central to the problem of these regions (Padoa-Schioppa, 1987, p. 163). Infrastructure is used in a broad sense to include transport facilities, public utilities like electricity generating stations, educational infrastructure and telecommunications (ibid., p. 168). The existing level of 'infrastructural endowment' in the five poorest EC countries is estimated and expressed as a percentage of the average for the EC 12; as Table 3.11 shows, countries like Portugal, Greece and Italy have an infrastructural endowment which is only 40–60 per cent of the EC average. Padoa-Schioppa then goes on to estimate the cost of a ten-year investment programme which

Table 3.11 Basic infrastructure needs in the least favoured regions

	Level of endowment hypothesis 1985 (EC 12 = 100)	Gap to index 80 (ECU/per capita)	Population (millions) 1985	10-year total (billion ECU)
Portugal	40	4,000	10.2	40.8
Greece	50	3,000	10.0	30.0
Spain	60	2,000	17.3	34.6
Ireland	60	2,000	3.6	7.2
Italy	60	2,000	20.3	40.6
Total				153.2

Source: Padoa-Schioppa (1987).

would close the gap and bring these countries up to a level of endowment equal to 80 per cent of the EC average. The total cost of the proposed investment programme is 153 billion ECU or roughly 15 billion ECU per annum for ten years.

If the Commission sponsored the Padoa-Schioppa programme of infrastructural improvement, the cost would not be met entirely, or even mainly, out of the structural funds. The EC specific purpose grants are 'matching grants'; national governments can only claim assistance from the structural funds for projects to which they commit national funds. By taking the case of Greece, we can examine the extent to which the Padoa-Schioppa programme would be funded from the structural funds as against funds from national exchequers; Greece is typical of the poorest EC countries, and the outcome would be similar in countries like Portugal.

The current upper limit on EC structural fund assistance to Greece can be fairly straightforwardly calculated. For the year 1989 we know the total sum available from the structural funds, and we can assume that Greece will get the same share of that total as it did in 1986; in that case, in 1989 Greece would receive 850 million ECU from the structural funds. The cost of implementing the Padoa-Schioppa programme for upgrading infrastructure in Greece is nearly 3 billion ECU a year. If the Greek government were to receive no more from the structural funds than it did in 1989, then the Greek government would have to find some 2.1 billion ECU a year from its own resources to finance infrastructural improvement. For the Greek economy, 2 billion ECU represents a very substantial sum; it is equivalent to roughly 85 per cent of public sector gross domestic capital formation and 12 per cent of total public expenditure in 1988. In fairness, it must be emphasised that the outcome may not be quite so dire, because the Commission proposes to enlarge the structural funds, and that would allow larger grants to Greece and, maybe, less drain on the national exchequer. But the enlargement of the structural funds depends on the successful containment of agricultural price-support expenditure which, as we have argued, is far from certain.

On the Padoa-Schioppa scenario, EC regional policy simultaneously provides assistance to national governments and makes large demands on public spending by national governments. These demands must be set in the context of public sector finance in the poorer countries and the attitude of the Commission towards 'irresponsible' public finance. As Table 3.12 shows, the poorer south European countries already have public sector deficits which are well in excess of the average for the EC 12 and very much larger than the deficits in the wealthier north European countries. The Commission's attitude to public sector deficits is unofficially expressed in the Padoa-Schioppa report, which deplores the existence of large deficits and argues that grants of resources from the structural funds should be conditional on the reduction of large deficits.

> Several of the poorest member states have public sector deficits of the order of 10 per cent of GDP or more which have a considerable structural component. These deficits need urgently to be set on a medium-term trajectory for reduction to sustainable levels. *It would be hard to justify the Community extending much increased budgetary assistance to these countries unless their macroeconomic strategies were simultaneously directed towards financial stability in the medium-term* (Padoa-Schioppa, 1987, p. 101, emphasis added).

This kind of conditionality has a simple logic. Unless the poorer countries can increase revenue, they must reduce the overall level of government expenditure to curb their public-sector deficits. At the same time, if something like the Padoa-Schioppa programme is enacted, the poorer countries would have to increase public spending on infrastructure. The implication is that there must be cuts in national expenditure outside the sphere of infrastructural investment, or put another way, the policy objects which are not favoured by liberal market economics will be starved of resources.

Table 3.12 Government net lending (+) or net borrowing (−) of selected EC countries (percentage of GDP), 1981–8

	Ireland	France	W. Germany	Greece	Spain	Italy	Portugal	UK	EC12
1981	−13.4	−1.9	−3.7	−11.0	−3.9	−11.3	−9.2	−2.6	−5.3
1982	−13.7	−2.8	−3.3	−7.7	−5.6	−11.3	−10.4	−2.5	−5.5
1983	−11.6	−3.2	−2.5	−8.3	−4.8	−10.6	−9.1	−3.3	−5.3
1984	−9.6	−2.8	−1.9	−10.0	−5.5	−11.5	−12.0	−3.9	−5.3
1985	−11.1	−2.8	−1.1	−13.6	−7.0	−12.5	−10.1	−2.7	−5.2
1986	−11.0	−2.9	−1.3	−10.8	−5.7	−11.4	−7.8	−2.4	−4.8
1987	−9.1	−2.5	−1.8	−9.5	−3.6	−10.5	−8.4	−1.4	−4.2
1988	−6.5	−1.9	−2.3	−12.1	−3.0	−10.0	−8.1	−0.3	−3.8

Source: European Economy (November 1988).

Table 3.13 Public expenditure in Greece (% of GNP)

	1979	1981	1985	1986
Total	39.1	48.2	58.4	56.9
General government	31.8	38.2	48.7	47.8
of which:				
Goods & services	18.5	20.5	25.0	23.8
Transfers & subsidies	13.3	17.7	23.7	24.0

Source: Survey of Greece, Paris, OECD, 1987.

Thus, through an expansion of regional policy, the Commission could acquire new powers to determine the direction of public spending in poorer member states. If these states are to receive resources from the structural funds, then their internal economic and social policies will be subject to Commission tutelage and liberal market discipline. The consequences for the poorest countries, like Greece, would be dramatic and reactionary.

As Table 3.13 shows, in Greece over the past decade there has been a sharp increase in the share of public-sector expenditure in GDP. The increase occurred because successive Greek national governments adopted policies which were contrary to liberal market principles. While the EC talked of 'social protection', the Greek national government did something about it. Employment was created in the public sector where real wages were increasing; between 1980 and 1985 the growth in the number of government employees averaged 3.5 per cent per annum, while real wages in the public sector increased by 4.5 per cent per annum. The social security system was upgraded through an extension of benefit coverage to those, such as farmers and returned emigrant workers, who had not been insurance contributors; expenditure on pensions increased from 7.3 per cent of GNP in 1979 to 13.3 per cent of GNP in 1985. Subsidies to essential services increased as public-sector price rises were restrained in a period of inflation; subsidies to public sector enterprises increased from 2 per cent of GNP in 1979 to 5.5 per cent in 1985. There is little scope for defending these policies by increasing government revenue. For political reasons farmers are likely to remain virtually exempt from tax; farmers currently contribute only 0.2 per cent of total income tax revenue, although they make up a quarter of the workforce and income from agriculture accounts for 18 per cent of national income. Unless the revenue side is transformed, an expansion of EC regional policy, as envisaged in Padoa-Schioppa, will deliver Greece into the hands of the Commission and create the conditions necessary for liberal market tutelage.

At the beginning of this chapter we made the point that regional policy has been seen on the left as a necessary 'social' dimension of EC policy. The Greek example shows that this identification is completely spurious. Some on the left may take comfort from the fact that the Padoa-Schioppa report, although sponsored by the Commission, does not represent official Commission policy. However, the disciplinary preoccupations of Padoa-Schioppa are manifest in other official Commission documents. In Chapter Five we discuss the Delors Report on monetary union which envisages 'precise', and ultimately 'binding', rules about 'the size of annual budget deficits and their financing'. In the next phase of EC policy, the liberal market programme is to be extended, the 'errant' are to be disciplined, and those who are likely to err are the poor. The regional policy of the Commission is not designed as a counter-weight to the liberal market programme and may, in the near future, function as a means of liberal market discipline.

Chapter 4
Pandora's Box: Restructuring and EC Competition Policy

The issue of restructuring has already been touched upon in Chapter Two, which disputed the Commission's claims that restructuring would realise economies of scale and benefit consumers. In this chapter we present our own analysis of restructuring, a process which primarily involves the transfer of ownership and control over blocks of production assets through merger and joint venture. On our broad interpretation the process of restructuring also includes direct investment by Japanese firms who are now setting up manufacturing plants in Europe.

The first half of this chapter is concerned to answer a series of questions about the future pattern and consequences of restructuring: Will restructuring through merger, joint venture and inward investment increase in the 1990s? What form will restructuring take? And will restructuring work to increase or decrease the inequalities which have arisen from differences in economic development and the operation of free trade inside Europe? Our answers to questions about the future of restructuring must necessarily be tentative. To limit and direct this speculation, we start with an examination of existing patterns of merger and joint venture and then develop an analysis of the conditions which will continue to determine the form and extent of restructuring.

The second half of this chapter is concerned with EC policy on mergers and joint ventures. Here the most important question is whether EC competition policy will be effective in controlling restructuring. To answer this question we first examine the EC's existing competition policy, operated under Articles 85 and 86 of the Treaty of Rome and then turn to examine the new regime for merger control proposed in the Tenth Directive. Our conclusion is that both the old and the new policies are inadequate and insufficiently relevant. Just as EC social and regional policy will not make things better, so EC competition policy cannot stop things getting worse if restructuring imposes a further burden of disadvantage on the Mediterranean countries and declining industrial areas.

Merger and joint venture now

Takeovers, especially large international takeovers, figure prominently on the business pages of Europe's newspapers. That is because big business dramas like the Benedetti siege of Société Générale or Nestlé's takeover of Rowntree make good news stories. Business page readers may therefore presume the whole of Europe is now in the middle of a major merger boom. The statistics on European merger and joint venture, however, tell a rather different story. They show the activity is only intense in some countries and sectors.

There is intense merger activity inside Britain, and the nature of this activity can be analysed if we examine the British MQ7 series on mergers and acquisitions. As Table 4.1 shows, acquisition in the UK was at a cyclical peak between 1986 and 1988, and the volume of activity was substantial; in both 1986 and 1987 UK companies spent around £15 billion on acquiring companies. But most of that activity involved the acquisition of UK companies by other UK companies. The table shows that the number of foreign companies acquired and expenditure on foreign acquisitions account for a relatively small part of British M and A activity; in 1986 UK companies spent £3.3 billion on foreign acquisitions, and in every previous year, the level of expenditure had been below £1 billion. Even more important from our point of view, British foreign acquisitions mainly take the form of the purchase of North American firms; as Table 4.1 shows, UK companies until 1987 typically bought just 10–25 EC companies each year at a cost which is usually below £50 million per annum. Even in 1987 the cost of EC acquisitions only formed about 10 per cent of total cost of foreign acquisitions. These figures are an incomplete record of British overseas M and A, because they only cover acquisitions which have a foreign exchange cost; they exclude acquisitions by foreign sub-

107

Table 4.1 Acquisitions and mergers in the UK, 1969-86

	(i) Total acquisitions[a]			(ii) Acquisition of foreign companies			(iii) Acquisition of EC companies[b]		
	No. acquiring	No. acquired	£m	No. acquiring	No. acquired	£m	No. acquiring	No. acquired	£m
1969	686	846	1,068.9	34	43	29.2	10	10	10.0
1970	629	793	1,122.5	46	52	105.7	21	24	33.4
1971	687	884	911.1	53	62	73.0	19	20	26.5
1972	928	1,210	2,531.6	69	85	90.4	44	49	50.6
1973	929	1,205	1,304.3	80	88	178.5	53	57	73.7
1974	427	504	508.4	49	53	120.6	29	30	65.2
1975	276	315	290.8	17	18	41.3	9	10	29.9
1976	315	353	448.1	17	17	64.6	5	5	4.9
1977	427	481	823.8	18	18	142.8	6	6	8.2
1978	484	567	1,139.5	29	30	349.5	10	11	21.1
1979	447	534	1,656.4	55	63	344.8	10	11	46.6
1980	404	469	1,475.4	51	51	941.0	12	12	138.7
1981	389	452	1,143.7	139	150	726.2	25	29	23.6
1982	399	463	2,205.5	92	95	770.3	10	10	23.8
1983	391	447	2,342.9	56	58	387.1	14	14	28.9
1984	508	568	5,473.8	67	74	816.4	14	14	31.1
1985	383	474	7,090.4	58	64	931.5	14	15	57.5
1986	529	696	14,934.7	78	89	3,333.1	12	13	69.6
1987	850	1,125	15,362.9	197	223	7,047.7	59	68	796.5
1988	902	1,224	22,123.0						

[a] Acquisitions include acquisitions of independent companies and mergers and purchases of subsidiaries from company groups.
[b] Includes Denmark and Eire after 1972, Greece after 1981, Spain and Portugal after 1985.
Source: Department of Trade and Industry, *MQ7 Expenditure on Acquisitions and Mergers of Industrial and Commercial Companies since 1964.*

sidiaries of British firms and acquisitions by British firms whose cost is covered by borrowing in the country where the acquisition is made. But the order of magnitudes is such that the overall conclusion is clear; only a small part of Britain's takeover activity spills over into continental Europe.

. The mainland Europeans are not generating much M and A activity of their own. The value and volume of merger activity are rising in countries like France, but it is still alleged that the UK has more takeovers than all the other 11 countries put together (*Financial Times*, 23 December 1988). These international mergers account for a rising proportion of deals, but according to the EC's own statistics, the international deals constituted only half of the largest deals in 1987–8 (*Financial Times*, 20 December 1988), and their share of all deals is certainly much lower. The first comprehensive statistics on European international merger were recently published by Peat, Marwick and McLintock (1989) in *KPMG Deal Watch*, and this snapshot for the year 1988 confirms the impressionistic claims and assertions made in the existing literature. Again, we can epitomise the activity by concentration on the pattern of acquisitions. As Table 4.2 shows, intra-European M and A is a relatively small-scale business: in 1988 all EC companies (including British ones) bought just 453 other EC companies, at a dollar cost of $11 billion.

European international M and A could also be fairly described as an offshore business. The mainland European companies, especially German companies, are relatively small-scale purchasers; in 1988 German companies bought just 37 non-German EC companies, at a dollar cost of $405 million. European international M and A is dominated by the British, who account for more than two-thirds of the value and volume of international purchases. The main international flows from Britain (as from all the mainland countries, except Italy) are to the United States; if three-quarters of the value of UK international purchases are made in North America, so are four-fifths of the value of German purchases and two-thirds of the value of French purchases.

It is altogether more difficult to measure joint ventures because this category bundles together a variety of diverse arrangements for pooled research and development, jointly owned or controlled manufacturing facilities and co-operation about distribution, which may include the swapping of finished products and/or specialisation in particular markets. Most of these joint-venture activities

Table 4.2 European international mergers and acquisitions in 1988

Purchases by	Value (US $ mill.)				Number of deals			
	EC	N.Am	RoW	Total	EC	N.Am	RoW	Total
France	3,772	7,310	80	11,162	70	61	12	143
W. Germany	405	2,308	39	2,752	37	45	17	99
Ireland	500	992	106	1,598	41	10	2	53
Italy	1,164	153	60	1,377	18	10	1	29
Netherlands	602	632	42	1,276	17	28	7	52
UK	4,411	33,361	6,758	44,530	245	505	134	884
EC other	235	986	8	1,229	25	15	6	46
EC total	11,089	45,742	7,093	63,924	453	674	179	1,306

Source: Peat, Marwick and McLintock (1989).

Table 4.3 Alliances between European and non-European high technology companies in 1987–8[a]

	Europe[b] → Europe	EC[c] → USA	USA[c] → EC	Japan → EC	Total
Takeovers and mergers	69	74	71	17 .	231
Joint ventures/ alliances other than mergers	134		94	42	270
Total	203		239	59	501

[a]Survey period runs from June 1987 to September 1988.
[b]These figures include alliances involving non-EC European companies from Finland, Sweden and Switzerland in 8 takeovers and 21 joint ventures.
[c]These figures put the country of initiating company first, although it is not always clear which was the initiating company in agreed bids.
Source: Farrands (1988).

are undramatic and under-reported, but preliminary indications suggest that joint ventures may well be more significant than the takeovers which catch the headlines. In a recent article, Farrands (1988) surveyed merger and joint venture 'alliances' between European and non-European high-tech companies on the basis of press reports in the *Financial Times* and other sources. The main results are summarised in Table 4.3.

Table 4.3 shows that in the high-tech sector, joint ventures outnumber takeovers by 2:1 amongst intra-European alliances. The division of joint-venture activity between different countries is equally interesting because joint-venture activity is much more evenly spread around the European countries than is the case with merger. The survey by Farrands records more joint-venture participation by British companies, with the Germans not far behind. This ranking is probably the result of reporting bias in the English-language sources used by Farrands. The importance of joint venture in most mainland European countries is understandable if takeovers are few and company identity is stable in mainland Europe; joint ventures then become the obvious way of accessing and pooling productive know-how or market strength.

In the argument so far, we have tried to generalise about European merger and joint venture. The final point which should be made is that the sectoral impact of merger and joint venture is very uneven. One major sector, electrical engineering and electronics, has already been completely transformed by restructuring. The technically weak indigenous European electronics industry has become increasingly reliant on joint ventures with Japanese companies; thus Thomson has a joint venture with JVC for the production of VCRs, and Olivetti plans to produce copiers, fax and laser printers with Canon. But the spectacular change comes from shifts in ownership and control of major indigenous producers. The transformation began in the mid-1980s with a restructuring of the white goods sector through a series of deals which included the purchase of Zanussi by Electrolux. It gathered pace in 1986–7 with two mega-mergers: Asea and Brown Boveri merged to create a company which was far and away Europe's largest in power generation; and CGE of France acquired ITT's telecomms business and became the world's second largest telecommunications group after AT and T. Then in 1988 and 1989, Britain's GEC escaped takeover by putting together a series of defensive joint-venture deals with CGE, Siemens and General Electric of America; if all three deals go through, the result will be an effective demerger of GEC which backs half the assets of Britain's largest manufacturing company into a series of joint ventures.

In other sectors, especially foodstuffs and chemicals, restructuring has not (yet) transformed the overall European structure of ownership and control, but change through merger and joint venture is a significant factor. In foodstuffs, the existing European majors are consolidating their position by acquiring smaller complementary businesses which extend the range of geographical and product markets in which they operate. Recent deals of this type include not only Nestlé's purchase of Rowntree but also Unilever's acquisition of Revilla in Spain and Gervais Danone's purchase of General Biscuit, the third largest biscuit producer in the world. The fragmented nature of the European food industry is such that there is considerable scope for restructuring, which will almost certainly include the building of new conglomerates with food and other interests, like the one which Benedetti already controls.

In chemicals the restructuring has taken a slightly different form, with one major defensive merger and an assortment of smaller deals which allow individual companies to buy themselves in and out of particular markets. The 1988 merger between Enichem and the chemical businesses of Montedison created an Italian company which was the eighth largest chemical company in the world and, more important, a Euro-company which was the equal of ICI and the big three German companies. The smaller deals include acquisitions like Akzo of Holland's purchase of the fine chemicals of Ferrosan or Rhone-Poulenc's purchase of the British company, May and Baker. Divestment has been equally important with, for example, Fisons (UK) and Novo (Denmark) selling off fertiliser and chemicals interests to concentrate resources on pharmaceuticals and agricultural biotechnology. The general story may be that merger and joint venture in Europe is on a small scale, but in sectors like chemicals and foodstuffs it is hardly all quiet on the M and A front.

Business strategy versus national institutions and policy

Against this background of significant differences between countries and sectors, it is interesting to ask the question: what next? Will M and A activity spread onto the mainland from its present centre in Britain? Will other sectors be transformed by restructuring, as electricals and electronics has been transformed? What will be the future balance between merger and joint venture? These questions are best answered by analysis of the conditions inside and outside business which both promote and constrain the expansion of merger and joint-venture activity. Our general argument is that a variety of ideological and real conditions inside European business are encouraging the development of company strategies in which merger is a major instrument. But the implementation of these strategies on mainland Europe is obstructed by a variety of national institutions and policies. The likely outcome is some merger plus a more general diversion of the forces of restructuring into joint venture.

Chapter Two argued that the importance of economic 1992 – the Commission's little package for the removal of non-tariff barriers – has been greatly exaggerated. At this point we should add that ideological 1992 – the hype surrounding the Commission's package – has become an important force for change in European business. The 1992 programme has not really changed very much outside most companies, but it has created a new awareness of the European market inside the companies. Firms are not only trying to find out how the 1992 changes affect their business, they are also identifying the broader opportunities and threats in the Europe of the 1990s. In a recent CBI survey, 200 British companies were asked what, if anything, they had done to prepare for 1992. Setting up a strategy review was the most popular course of action amongst the 139 companies who had done something about 1992; 39 companies had set up a strategy review. The conclusions of strategy reviews depend, of course, on prevailing managerial ideologies. The next step in our argument is, therefore, to analyse these ideologies and their implications.

Business school gurus (e.g. Porter, 1987) now recommend concentration of resources on core businesses which aim for international or world leadership. In a popular management text, Peters and Waterman tell companies to 'stick to the knitting'; 'least successful as a general rule are those companies that diversify into a wide range of fields' (Peters and Waterman, 1982, p. 294). The prescription is that smaller companies should concentrate on niche markets and big companies should aim for more broadly based leadership in a few major product markets. This encourages restructuring because concentration of resources on core businesses can only be achieved quickly through a process of acquisition and divestment. Leaders of big business should be cautious about strategies which lead towards more-intense oligopolistic competition, but many of them are clearly directly influenced by the business school injunctions. Consider, for example, the case of Alain Gomez, the Harvard Business School educated chairman of the nationalised French concern Thomson. Under Gomez, Thomson has concentrated on consumer electronics and defence contracting by selling peripheral businesses and making bold new acquisitions. In consumer electronics, Thomson bought the RCA television business from GE of America and the Ferguson television business from Thorn, while the company's technical base in semi-conductor technology has been defended by a joint venture with the Italian company SGS and the purchase of the British chip company, Inmos, again from Thorn. In a recent interview, Gomez provided an explanation and a justification:

> The main lines of my strategy since I came here (in 1982) were to get relevant market positions whenever and wherever it was possible. And, if not possible, get out. That explains all the divestiture and concentration. We had 23 basic businesses in 1982 and now we are left with two major ones. (*Financial Times*, 30 January 1988)

Gomez may be unusually articulate, but many big companies are making similar calculations and taking action on them; the strategy

114

of Jack Welch at GE of America has been to concentrate on 14 key businesses.

In conjunction with ideological 1992, the fashion for core businesses is promoting a change in the focus of the strategies of major European manufacturers. These companies are no longer focusing their strategies on their domestic national markets. They are developing international strategies in a world where the Japanese majors, just like the American multinationals, already have global strategies. But the new European international strategies can only be implemented quickly when (or if) there are companies for sale at a reasonable price. The restructuring of the European electrical and electronics sector was rapid and total because, for a variety of sector-specific reasons, there were companies for sale. Power generation is a business plagued by a dearth of orders and 70-percent manufacturing over-capacity (*Financial Times*, 28 December 1988). In telecomms, the problem has been the cost of developing the next generation of electronic PABX equipment. Furthermore, several significant players like GEC and Plessey were quoted on the British stock market and vulnerable to hostile takeover. But in other sectors, like motor cars, only minor companies like Alfa and SEAT have been sold in the 1980s, and all the majors are firmly not for sale. For example, Renault's shares are held by the French government and VW's by German banks, while Ford and GM's European operations are the wholly-owned subsidiaries of American parents who want to buy not sell. The pressure on the more economically vulnerable majors eased when the car market turned up in the mid-1980s and it became easier to finance development costs from increased profits. The restructuring of European cars will probably only happen when the Japanese have put in enough European manufacturing capacity to threaten (or panic) the weaker majors.

At a micro level, it is true that the volume and value of M and A is a matter of variable and contingent circumstances in each business sector. But the framework of national financial institutions is the more important macro determinant of the number of companies sold in each country. Merger only becomes a frantic, general activity in (and between) economies which meet two general preconditions: first, there must be a well-developed stock exchange where most large companies are quoted on the secondary market; second, the dominant investors must have no fixed loyalty to existing managements, so that investors make purely financial calculations about the management of their portfolios. In national economies where these two preconditions are met, as in Britain and America, the consent of the acquired company is not required, and hostile takeover is an ever-present possibility. But the three big mainland national economies, Germany, France and Italy, do not clearly meet the key institutional preconditions. In Germany, for example, there are only 800 companies with a status equivalent to British PLCs, and German investors, like banks and insurance companies, have traditionally made a long-term commitment to the companies they invest in. In Britain, by way of contrast, institutional and private investors are preoccupied with short-term dealing profits, and it is almost always possible for a takeover raider to buy into a company by ringing fund managers and offering a 50 or 100p premium over yesterday's close; the Rowntree affair began when Suchard effortlessly bought 13.7 per cent of the company in one 'dawn raid'.

If institutional conditions constrain merger on the mainland, these effects are reinforced because, in many European countries, national policy puts further obstacles in the way of takeover. National policy regulations on merger vary considerably between countries (see Cooke, 1988). At one extreme, in Italy, there are no set rules and no official agency charged with vetting mergers and takeovers. But in the largest economy, Germany, there is a powerful regulatory agency which is suspicious of mergers that abridge competition. The Bundeskartellamt can intervene to block mergers and joint ventures, as it did in 1984 when it prevented Philips from forming a joint venture with Siemens for the production of optical fibres. Furthermore, in several EC economies, national legislation allows various forms of permanent defence against hostile takeover. In Holland, for example, the works council has a right of appeal to the courts in cases where the council opposes a transfer of ownership; under Dutch law, it is also possible to create a class of 'priority shareholders', whose consent is required before ownership can change hands. In West Germany, companies can secure themselves defensively by restricting the voting rights attached to newly-acquired shares (*Financial Times*, 23 December 1988). Finally, only the British government takes a clear and unequivocal line on international free trade in company ownership, a line which was strongly reasserted at the time of the Rowntree takeover. Most mainland European governments are suspicious of, or hostile to, foreign takeover of major domestic companies. The British publisher, Pearson, for example, had to obtain French government approval before its £88 million agreed bid for Les Echos could go ahead.

The institutional and policy framework leaves British companies unusually open to takeover by mainland European companies, which are in varying degrees bid-proof. But as Table 4.4 shows, few EC companies have exercised this option. American companies, in the 'other countries' category, account for most of the acquisition of British companies by foreign companies; in the period 1980–6 EC companies bought on average 5 British companies each year at an average annual cost of £67.8 million. Within the free-trade EC, mainland companies can manufacture at home and sell in Britain through a wholly-owned distribution network. And while British companies may have home market share, most of them do not have other competitive advantages which would make them attractive purchases. Why then should an EC company trouble to acquire a British manufacturing operation and struggle to integrate the British factory into an international network? That option is only necessary or advantageous in highly visible and politically sensitive areas like defence contracting or high unit-value consumer goods. Thus, in cars, Peugeot bought the old Rootes business in Coventry from Chrysler, and VW wanted to buy Austin Rover. In consumer electronics Thomson bought Ferguson from Thorn, and in defence contracting Siemens is involved with GEC in a joint bid for Plessey. Through such deals, a foreign company can acquire a politically acceptable British face. No doubt this cosmetic trade will continue, but there is no obvious reason why it should expand greatly.

In the mainland countries, the institutional framework and national policy will continue to inhibit free-for-all merger and acquisition on the British pattern. These macro-constraints will not, however, prevent merger in sectors, like electricals and electronics, where firms are under pressure because of sector-specific problems. More generally, there will be room for a few Euro-takeover specialists like Benedetti. And a continuous steady trickle of sales by British companies and American multinationals is enough to allow French companies to play at international strategy. But a wholesale Euro-merger boom seems unlikely, and in our view, this blockage will encourage the further development of joint ventures as the only form of alliance which can incorporate bid-proof companies. Consider, for example, the actions and calculations of GEC's Lord Weinstock. GEC is a cash-rich company

Table 4.4 Acquisition of UK companies by foreign companies, 1969–86

	Total			EC countries[a]			Other countries		
	No. acquiring	No. acquired	£m	No. acquiring	No. acquired	£m	No. acquiring	No. acquired	£m
1969	27	27	58.2	2	2	1.0	25	25	57.2
1970	23	23	57.2	1	1	0.3	22	22	56.9
1971	19	21	32.7	2	2	0.5	17	19	32.2
1972	18	18	41.4	1	1	0.2	17	17	41.2
1973	5	8	58.0	1	1	9.0	4	7	49.0
1974	9	9	184.9	2	2	6.2	7	7	178.7
1975	9	9	53.5	2	3	4.7	6	6	48.8
1976	10	10	72.8	1	1	8.6	9	9	64.2
1977	12	12	79.5	3	3	1.3	9	9	78.2
1978	13	13	38.6	3	5	11.3	8	8	27.3
1979	6	6	47.1	3	3	6.1	3	3	41.0
1980	23	23	169.7	6	6	27.2	17	17	142.4
1981	72	75	493.4	12	14	36.3	60	61	457.1
1982	29	29	229.6	4	4	3.2	25	25	226.4
1983	20	20	187.5	1	1	115.5	19	19	72.0
1984	26	28	512.2	1	1	–	25	27	512.2
1985	21	21	223.6	3	3	34.5	18	18	189.1
1986	27	27	509.6	7	7	257.9	20	20	251.6

[a]EC includes Denmark and Eire after 1972, Greece after 1981 and Spain and Portugal after 1985.
Source: Department of Trade and Industry, *British Business. Cross Border Acquisitions and Mergers,* various years.

which can afford a major acquisition, and its key strategic move at the beginning of the 1980s was an attempt to take over AEG. That deal was blocked by opposition from German business and union interests; AEG went to Daimler Benz. GEC's next major move was a series of joint ventures with its competitors in the late 1980s. Lord Weinstock justified these joint ventures with the argument that Europe was not ready for large-scale acquisition:

> You cannot go out with £1.5 billion and buy a company of the magnitude that we need to make any change in the status quo [in electrical engineering] . . . so you have the option of adding bits piecemeal or doing something bolder. And that means coming to [joint venture] arrangements. (*Financial Times*, 30 December 1988)

Of course, he would say that, wouldn't he? Joint ventures are a defensive necessity for a British quoted company whose profits have faltered and whose technical base has atrophied. But the survey evidence shows that many European businessmen, who are not at risk of takeover, are making the same calculation as Lord Weinstock about joint venture. A recent KPMG survey of 700 businessmen, across all the EC countries, found that two-thirds of companies were considering some form of 'association' with companies in other EC countries (*Financial Times*, 3 January 1989). This is the way the pre-1992 world of European business will end: not with a bang (or a whimper) but with a licensing agreement.

The consequences of restructuring

It is difficult to predict the consequences of restructuring, because no existing body of discourse provides the key to understanding these processes of change. There is very little theory or experience of joint venture, and as we argue below, neither economics nor history provides us with a basis for predicting the consequences of Euro-mergers.

Economists insert mergers into their problematic of consumer welfare: mergers are either a good thing, because they benefit consumers through the realisation of productive efficiency, or they are a bad thing because they harm consumers through an increase in market power which raises prices (or reduces variety). The polar positions on Euro-merger are represented by the Cecchini Report and Geroski's article, which were considered in the discussion of restructuring in Chapter Two. Here we need do no more than

119

summarise the arguments developed in that discussion. Even within the limits of the consumer welfare problematic, neither Cecchini nor Geroski is convincing. The EC's hope that mergers will realise greater efficiency rests on an appeal to the unreal concept of economies of scale, with no clear specification of how these economies will be realised. Geroski's fear that Euro-merger will lead to a reduction of diversity and 'large Euro firms producing mass European goods on a large scale' (Davis et al., 1989, p. 38) is equally unreal because there is no hard evidence that larger firms will reduce the diversity of products offered.

If formal economics provides no convincing predictions, it is possible to appeal to historical experience. The British economy provides recent case material on the consequences of large-scale merger activity. Although it is too early to judge the results of the 1980s merger boom, the evidence is in on the earlier boom of the 1960s in which nearly half of British quoted companies were taken over. These mergers were generally unsuccessful in that the profitability of the merged companies was lower than that of the independent companies before merger (Meeks, 1977). As we have argued elsewhere (Williams et al., 1983), the most plausible explanation is that merger increased spans of control and encouraged a self-defeating preoccupation with managing production through financial controls. The practical result was BLMC/BL and GEC. But the problem with this appeal to history is that we cannot know whether the future will be like the past. The failing giant firms operated under British management in British institutional conditions. It is not clear that a new generation of Euro-giants would be so institutionally handicapped or so incompetently managed. They could do better.

The indeterminacy of orthodox economic and historical argument is such that it is worth trying a different approach to predicting consequences. Let us begin by conceding that restructuring through mergers and joint ventures does not have a simple internal logic which produces invariant effects. Much will depend on the context in which restructuring occurs. If we define that context in micro- and macro-economic terms, it should be possible to say something about the choices and decisions facing the managers of restructured enterprises. By pursuing this line of argument, it is also possible to bring the discussion round to the issue of restructuring and producer welfare and to bring the unseen of orthodox welfare economics into the area of the visible.

Table 4.5 Labour productivity (value added per man) differentials
between some major industrial countries

	UK	France	Germany	USA	Japan
Strong demand sectors					
Electricals/electronic	28	47	43	100	236
Office & data processing	37	43	45	100	94
Chemicals, etc.	54	79	75	100	119
Moderate demand sectors					
Transport equipment	23	54	60	100	95
Food/beverages/tobacco	56	73	47	100	37
Paper/printing	43	67	76	100	89
Industrial machinery	20	49	46	100	103
Weak demand sectors					
Metal products/ferrous	38	60	54	100	143
Metal products/non-ferrous	66	72	92	100	149
Textiles/clothing	59	62	71	100	53
Non-metallic	40	64	71	100	43
Total	42	65	65	100	100

Source: EC (1988), p. 28.

We can begin our alternative analysis by considering the micro-
economic enterprise level context. At a micro level, much depends
on whether European firms can improve efficiency and move up
the world rankings by closing the efficiency gap with Japan. As
Table 4.5 shows, Japanese labour productivity is well ahead of
European labour productivity in most sectors; the Europeans are
only competitive in a few traditional sectors like clothing and food
processing. If the Europeans can close the gap, then (with or
without restructuring) all things are possible. Increased competitiveness would shift demand constraints by allowing European
firms to take a larger share of the world market, as their Japanese
counterparts did in the 1970s and the 1980s.

Engineers and consultants (e.g. Schonberger, 1982; and Hartley,
1987) have provided accessible accounts of Japanese principles of
production management; others have analysed Japanese marketing.
But putting the principles into practice to close the efficiency gap is
turning out to be unexpectedly difficult. Some major companies,
like Ford of Europe, have tried and failed. This company has
achieved significant improvements through 'After Japan' pro-

grammes in some areas: press die change times have been reduced to between three and four-and-a-half hours. But the company is nowhere near Japanese standards of performance: on similar equipment, leading Japanese firms can change the dies in around 10 minutes. Because Ford's European assembly plants cannot be operated at Japanese levels of efficiency, the company is now trying to win efficiency improvements by a dramatic simplification of the assembly task. In 1989 (*Financial Times*, 30 January 1989) the company announced that each of its major assembly plants would in future produce just one model; this amounts to an admission of defeat in plants like Dagenham where millions of pounds have been spent on flexible automated body lines which were designed to handle all the variants of two entirely different models. Given the difficulty of managing change, it is not surprising that we can find individual cases of failed Japanisation. But it is altogether more worrying that, right across European manufacturing, there is, in the aggregate, no sign of effective Japanisation.

Japanese manufacturing practice puts considerable emphasis on the integration of manufacturing processes and the reduction of stock levels. The aim of stock reduction is both to expose physical problems, such as process bottlenecks, inside the factory and to cut costs by eliminating the indirect labour which handles stocks. Survey evidence (Ingersoll, 1987) shows that the British are having no success with stock reduction. As British factories have long been peculiarly disorganised, this is not unexpected. But census of production data on stock levels in national manufacturing sectors shows that the Germans are no more successful than the British in taking stocks out. Table 4.6 presents the basic data for Britain, Germany and Japan; as an aid to comparison, the value of stocks is calculated as the equivalent of so many weeks of final sales. As the table shows, there are significant cyclical variations in all the manufacturing sectors, and the level of stocks is consistently lower in Germany than in Britain. But there is no evidence of a secular reduction in stock levels in German manufacturing which would close the gap with Japan.

It would not be sensible to expect a sudden, spectacular reduction in European stock levels; after all, it took the clever Japanese 15 years to take out three weeks sales cover between 1955 and 1969, and they have not managed any consistent further improvement since then. But our analysis of the conditions of stock reduction in Japan makes us pessimistic about whether the Europeans will in the

Table 4.6 Stock cover in British, German and Japanese manufacturing, 1970–85

	Japan No. of weeks stock (i)	W. Germany No. of weeks stock (ii)	UK No. of weeks stock (iii)
1970	6.6	9.0	10.2
1971	7.0	9.4	n.a
1972	6.5	9.1	n.a
1973	6.4	8.8	10.4
1974	7.2	9.1	10.0
1975	8.4	10.0	10.8
1976	7.3	9.6	10.6
1977	7.1	9.0	10.8
1978	6.6	9.1	11.1
1979	6.2	9.0	10.6
1980	6.5	9.4	11.6
1981	6.6	9.5	11.8
1982	6.7	9.5	11.3
1983	6.3	9.1	10.6
1984	5.9	8.6	10.0
1985	5.6	n.a	9.3

Sources: Column (i), Statistics Bureau Co-ordination Agency, *Japan Statistical Yearbook*, 'Business Enterprise Survey', turnover of inventory in manufacturing, Tokyo, various years.
Column (ii), *Industrial Statistics Yearbook 1985*, Vol. 1, General Industrial Statistics, United Nations, New York, 1987.
Column (iii) *Report on Census of Production* (PA1002), HMSO, London, various years.

medium term achieve current Japanese standards. Stock reduction requires a physical mastery of production; problems about plant layout, machine reliability and line imbalance must be identified and solved. Our case work on Japanese car press shops (Williams et al., 1989b) suggests that stock reduction also requires a committed workforce that will do whatever is necessary to achieve improvement targets. If the capability of German production engineers is not in question, we believe German workers will not (and should not) cede an infinite prerogative to management. German unions are the strongest in Europe; at firms like VW reorganisations of production have to be negotiated with I.G. Metall. Many European firms claim they are winning increased 'flexibility' from their workforces, but this flexibility does not include Japanese practices like work to finish the production quota, individualised wage rates

123

and the collective punishment of large work groups if individuals or small groups resist improvement targets.

The cultural difference and the strength of organised labour may provide some shelter for European firms inside Europe because it puts a floor under competition; the implication of our argument is that Japanese companies will find it difficult to replicate Japanese standards of performance in their new European factories. But if European firms cannot improve world competitiveness, their share of world markets cannot be secure. Against this micro-economic background, European restructuring can be characterised as a defensive response which does not address the unsolved problem; it is hard to see how transfers of ownership and changes in the management team will solve general problems about competitiveness which are rooted in the organisation of production. Restructuring would not be the answer to Euro-sclerosis, as the EC supposes; it would more often be the reformulation of the problem 'under new management'. This pessimism is reinforced when we analyse the macro-economic context in which the restructuring of the 1990s will take place.

Restructuring in an expanding national or regional economy, where demand is growing and output can easily be sold, will have very different effects from restructuring in a stagnant economy, where demand falters and output cut-backs are required. The giant firms created by merger in the 1950s and 1960s in Britain only ran into dire problems when the long world boom gave out, the national macro-climate grew colder and recessionary shocks battered British manufacturing; the first recession after 1973 triggered a profits crisis, and in the second slump after 1979 there was a wave of bankruptcies and redundancies as real manufacturing output fell by nearly 20 per cent. We would not risk a prediction about a world recession in the 1990s, and nobody can know whether the cyclical upswing of the late 1980s will turn down into a major recession. But it is likely that for at least part of the 1990s the regional economic climate of Europe will be unfavourable. As we argued in Chapter One, the European economy has internal structural problems of imbalance which will constrain expansion unless and until the Germans change their policies. For this reason, there are likely to be hard times ahead for European manufacturing in the 1990s. Restructuring in hard times by European firms, which cannot improve their world competitiveness, is likely to be a euphemism for retrenchment and redundancy.

Table 4.7 Vintage of real gross capital stock in major European
manufacturing countries and US, 1965–83

	percentage share of assets aged 5 years or less			
	1965	1970	1975	1983
W. Germany	49.5	45.9	41.5	39.2
Italy	42.4	34.7	36.5	27.9
France	46.4	44.4	41.8	33.8
UK	29.0	28.9	24.8	18.7
US	40.7	47.6	43.2	45.5

Source: Economic Survey of Europe 1986–7, Geneva, United Nations, p. 89.

Our argument about the micro- and macro-economic context of
restructuring takes us away from the orthodox economists' question about whether consumers will benefit. It brings us to a more
serious question about where producers will lose their jobs. It is
impossible to say how many manufacturing workers will lose their
jobs through restructuring. But we can say something about whose
factories will close and where the blows will fall. Britain, the
laggard of northern Europe, is likely to lose out yet again in any
process of restructuring. Whether closure decisions are determined
by economic calculation or company politics, Britain is peculiarly
vulnerable.

Rational economic restructuring requires the closure of the most
inefficient plants so that their output can be transferred to existing
or enlarged plants which are more efficient. The national manufacturing sectors which lose out through this kind of restructuring will
be those which have a disproportionate share of inefficient plants.
As Table 4.5 showed, there are large differences in labour productivity between European countries, and a disproportionate
share of the low productivity is still concentrated in Britain. In all
but one of the eleven manufacturing sectors, British value added
per man is lower than value added per man in Germany and France;
it is also the case that the margin of British inferiority is larger in the
strong and moderate demand sectors. If the logic of productivity
differentials requires closure in Britain, that logic is reinforced by
age of plant. The installed capacity in British manufacturing is not
only less productive, it is also substantially older. Table 4.7 shows
that installed capacity in western Europe is now generally of more
elderly vintage than it was twenty years ago. Then as now, British
manufacturing's capacity is more antiquated than that of our com-

petitors; currently, less than 20 per cent of British manufacturing's capital stock is less than five years old, compared with nearly 40 per cent of the capital stock in German manufacturing.

It is true that modest depreciation charges and relatively low wages may be offsetting operating advantages for British factories. But these will not be worth very much if the closure decisions are a matter of company politics rather than straightforward economic calculation. The Commission dreams of the creation of 'truly European' companies which have no links to a particular country and are thus able to escape from the 'national champion mentality' (EC, 1988, p. 135). The idea that we shall get 'European companies' flies in the face of the whole history of multinational companies; although there are cases of multinational enterprises (like Unilever) with joint bases, there is no example of a company with no national base. And Britain has political cause to fear restructuring because the process is likely to create large operating units whose headquarters and main factories are on the mainland. This trend is already clear. The GEC/CGE (Alsthom) joint venture backed around one-quarter of GEC's turnover and 42,000 British employees into a business whose head office will be in Paris and whose chief executive will be French (*Financial Times*, 28 December 1988). If the Carnaud/Metal Box deal in packaging goes ahead, CMB packaging will have its headquarters in Brussels and operations throughout Europe (*Financial Times*, 27 October 1988). The new continental bosses may do a better job of operating the old British factories, but if it comes to closure, they may well also do a more brutal job. The company politics of plant closure often lead to the closure of branch factories (regardless of efficiency or industrial relations record) so that the central manufacturing facilities can be defended. If merger and joint venture gather pace, British manufacturing will have a disproportionate number of vulnerable branch factories.

The argument so far suggests that restructuring is likely to reinforce rather than counterweight the centralisation of production. This may seem unnecessarily negative if restructuring involves not only the closure of old factories but also direct investment to start new factories. The optimists would point to Japanese inward investment in manufacturing start-ups; with the expansion of direct exports from Japan likely to be blocked, the Japanese have no choice but to produce inside fortress Europe. It is often supposed that this is a source of advantage which can transform

Table 4.8 Destinations of Japanese foreign direct investment (cumulative total to April 1987)

	North America	Latin America	Asia	Europe	Total
Manufacturing investment ($ mill.)	14,753	4,994	10,000	3,310	36,036
Non-manufacturing investment ($ mill.)	36,858	20,126	16,286	16,794	99,365

Source: *Financial Times*, 15 November 1988.

performance in the laggard and underdeveloped countries. For example, before the 1979 British general election, there were informal discussions at a senior level inside the Labour Party about the possibility of an industrial strategy of 'handing over manufacturing to the Japanese'. Just as the US cavalry charged over the hill to save the settlers in the last reel of the old B-movie Westerns, so the Japanese will turn up just in time to save the peripheral countries and the declining industrial regions. The problem is that a happy ending is hardly guaranteed when the Japanese are so far only coming over the hill in small infantry detachments.

The arrival of Japanese manufacturing in Europe is an event of considerable symbolic importance and general interest. And European firms, in sectors like electronics and cars, are understandably preoccupied by the Japanese threat to their profits and market share. But the fact is that the flow of Japanese direct investment into European manufacturing has so far been a trickle, not a torrent. As Table 4.8 shows, over the past twenty years, most Japanese direct investment in manufacturing has gone into the countries of the Pacific basin. More than two-thirds of the cumulative total has gone to Asia and North America; less than 10 per cent (or just $3 billion) went into European manufacturing. The proportion going to Europe has been rising in recent years, but in 1987 Europe still took only 20 per cent of all Japanese foreign direct investment (Nomura Research, 1988).

For the past twenty years, direct investment in Europe has had a low priority because, for Japanese manufacturing, Europe is a relatively unimportant market halfway round the world; in 1987 Europe took only 17 per cent of Japanese exports whereas the US market alone took 38 per cent (Nomura Research, 1988). In North

127

America in the 1980s, direct investment has been used as a back-up way of consolidating important market positions, which Japanese direct exports had already captured. Japanese investment priorities are, however, changing, and the volume of Japanese direct investment in European manufacturing is likely to increase dramatically over the next few years. With capacity in place in North America, Japanese manufacturers can now turn to Europe, and the 'fortress Europe' panic encourages companies like Toyota to believe that European manufacture will become the only way of securing access to the European market. But if the trickle of Japanese direct investment in the 1980s grows into a torrent in the 1990s, that will not transform the laggard economy of Britain or develop the Mediterranean countries.

Increases in Japanese manufacturing activity will initially take the form of large percentage increases from very small bases. In 1987, there were just 274 Japanese manufacturing establishments in Europe as a whole (Nomura Research, 1988); Britain, the country with the largest number, had just 67 (ibid.). Most of the Japanese establishments are very small and employ only a few hundred workers. The new Japanese car plants are going to be operations of a rather different kind. But they will be very much smaller than the largest European assembly plants like VW Wolfsburg or Fiat Mirafiori. Nissan, Toyota and Mazda each have a European assembly plant in operation or in preparation: each of these plants will have a capacity of just 200,000 cars a year (*Wall Street Journal*, Europe, 23 March 1989). The Japanese plants in Europe could be fairly represented as relatively small-scale social and economic experiments.

If the experiments are successful, then the plants will be extended. But it should not be assumed that Japanese majors will always, or usually, aim for a massive expansion of their European manufacturing operations. Japanese technological leadership can be most profitably and securely exploited in Europe by some combination of direct exports from Japan, local manufacture and joint ventures with established European firms. In electronics, the Japanese have leadership in many technologies and product areas along with an established European production base. But there is no sign that the Japanese are aggressively attacking European majors like Olivetti, Philips and Thomson in a way which would drive these firms out of manufacturing. Even if we assume that the Japanese plan will include local volume manufacture for many mass markets, that will bring relatively little benefit to the peripheral south

European economies. The Japanese prefer to spread their manufacturing plants around the high-income markets of northern Europe; in 1987, two-thirds of all Japan's European manufacturing establishments were in France, West Germany and the UK (Nomura Research, 1988). Up to the present Britain has had a larger number of Japanese plants than any other European country. The language factor and relatively low wages, together with government support and aid packages, all pull the Japanese to Britain. But the effect of these factors should not be exaggerated: in 1987 the British had 67 Japanese plants, the Germans had 60 (ibid.).

EC policy on joint venture and merger

Our argument so far suggests that the volume of merger and joint venture activity will increase in the 1990s, and the consequence is likely to be an increase in the centralisation of production. At the same time there are strong reasons for believing that, despite this, European firms will still fail to close the efficiency gap with Japan. If the results of restructuring are mixed and the benefits less than overwhelming, it is reasonable to ask whether the Commission has powers which are adequate to control international alliances through merger and joint venture.

This question is neither posed nor answered in the official literature on 1992. It is a central question both in its own right and because, as we saw in Chapter Two, restructuring accounts for most of the postulated Stage Two gains. But restructuring can be double-edged in its effects on prices and competition. The official literature thus concedes that control of restructuring is necessary. As we have already observed in Chapter Two, Cecchini discriminates between good and bad mergers and thereby sets up a distinction between two kinds of restructuring. In good restructuring through merger and collaboration, enterprises realise productive efficiency (via economies of scale), and competitive pressures ensure the gains are passed on to consumers. In bad restructuring, merger and joint venture are used to defend inefficient enterprises and restrict competition. Cecchini warns that enterprises may 'seek various forms of shelter from competitive reinvigoration' via the creation of dominant positions, potentially leading to abuses like barriers to new entry to the market, market sharing and discriminatory behaviour (Cecchini, 1988, p. 90). Without any form of justification, it is blandly assumed that good restructuring will predominate before and after 1992. There is no attempt to argue that market mechanisms automatically ensure this outcome. And there is no discussion of whether, and, if so, how, the Commission could enforce the predominance of good restructuring.

The whole question of whether and how industrial restructuring should be policed is increasingly disputed. Traditional 'anti-trust' policies embody a general presumption in favour of competition and against monopoly; collusion between independent firms is always wrong, and mergers which increase market power are usually dubious. But this presumption is now under challenge from both the right and the left. The radical right argues that merger should be decided by shareholders rather than government regulators. Economists, like Baumol (1965), argue for a free market in company ownership, where takeover and threat of takeover discipline inefficient management. Even if this kind of restructuring creates a dominant market share, that will not lead to abuse if barriers to entry are low. The centre and centre-left argue the case for new kinds of regulatory framework in which the desirability of competition is balanced against other considerations, such as the requirements of industrial policy (see, e.g., Cowling, 1987). The argument is that, if a government wishes to ensure that new technologies are exploited or key firms are internationally competitive, it may be necessary to condone high market shares or abridgements of competition.

Even if general criteria for condoning abridgements of competition can be settled, it is extraordinarily difficult to develop and apply a relevant and coherent policy on restructuring. The measurement of market power is not easy when the private corporation has become a diversified, multi-product, giant firm operating internationally across a range of product markets where it holds different shares. This opens the way for endless legal sophistry about whether product markets should be defined broadly or narrowly and how substitute products should be treated. If policy is to be relevant, it must inspect and rule on all forms of restructuring in firms above a minimum size. And policy is only coherent if all forms of collusion and cooperation between independent firms, as well as merger, are treated according to one set of criteria. Coherence is necessary to establish the basic principle of similar treatment for functionally equivalent arrangements. Given the diversity of forms which restructuring can take, it is much easier to state these prerequisites than to satisfy them. But if they are not satisfied, then the policing of restructuring is likely to be ineffectual. Where policy on the abridgement of competition is irrelevant or incoherent, firms will simply choose the forms of restructuring which are condoned and allowed. This kind of opportunism can only be prevented by regulatory agencies which operate carefully drafted regulations and clear-cut procedures.

The Commission does not have this advantage in the regulation of European restructuring. It is still trying to obtain agreement on a new regulation and directive on international mergers. Meanwhile, the Commission must try to control international restructuring by applying Articles 85 and 86 of the Treaty of Rome, which were designed to prevent the abridgement of competition. Much depends on the interpretation of the relevant articles in the European Court. But the basics are fairly straightforward. Joint venture, like collusion between independent firms, is dealt with under Article 85, which prohibits practices whose object or effect is to 'prevent, restrict or distort competition in the Common Market'. Article 85 does not necessarily completely prohibit such practices because, under Article 85(3), an agreement which abridges competition can be exempted if it 'contributes to improving the production or distribution of goods or to promoting technical progress'. Exemption is subject to various conditions: the agreement concerned should allow consumers 'a fair share of the benefits concerned'; restrictions on competition must be limited to those which are indispensable to the objects concerned; and the agreement must not allow the parties to eliminate competition entirely. Mergers have usually been dealt with under Article 86, which states that 'any abuse by one or more undertakings of a dominant position within the Common Market or a substantial part of it shall be incompatible with the Common Market in so far as it may affect trade between member states.' Although Article 86 has been used for merger control, the article does not explicitly refer to mergers. It can only be used to control mergers which strengthen (rather than create) a dominant position, and abuse may have to occur before intervention is possible. Finally, in Article 86 there is no provision, corresponding to Article 85(3), for selective exemption of mergers which strengthen a dominant position but are desirable on other grounds.

On closer examination the EC's existing policy towards restructuring under Articles 85 and 86 is thoroughly incoherent and irrelevant. Restructuring is not controlled according to one set of criteria, and much restructuring is effectively uncontrolled. Joint venture is freely allowed because the Article 85(3) exemption is given considerable weight in the decisions of the Commission and the judgements of the European Court. This is incoherent when collusion between independent firms is severely punished by the Commission. Policy on merger is largely irrelevant because Article 86 does not allow the Commission to frame a policy which covers most large international mergers. As for the proposed new merger control regulation, that will deliver much less than the Commission promises. The effect of the new merger regulation may well be to make international merger easier, not more difficult. In relation to business restructuring, the Commission is not so much a policeman, more a bent copper who encourages the activities which he should stop. At all events what we see in practice in the EC is the Commission engaged in a stringent and ruthless pursuit of covert price fixing and market sharing but extending toleration to almost every other form of cooperation between independent firms.

The simplest form of cooperation between independent firms is collusion to fix prices or output quotas. And the Commission has taken an extremely hard line on such arrangements. As we have seen, Article 85 of the Treaty of Rome is concerned with collusion between independent firms and practices which 'prevent, restrict or distort competition'. And under Article 85, the Commission has pursued a highly active policy of imposing large fines on international cartels which engage in price fixing and market sharing. As Swann (1988, p. 120) observes, 'the record is extremely impressive – virtually no cartel with significant market power has been exempted'. For example, the Commission recently imposed a record fine of 60 million ECU on 23 west European chemical companies, including Enichem, BASF, Bayer, ICI and BP (*Financial Times*, 22 December 1988). These companies had responded to recession and overcapacity by forming a cartel which maintained a list of 'posted prices' and organised market sharing in low density polyethylene and polyvinylchloride (PVC); the cartel had included all the major European producers of polyethylene and PVC, who jointly had an 80 per cent plus share of the market. This was not the first time that the majors in European chemicals have had to pay swingeing fines for organising price fixing and market sharing; in 1986 a 57.8 million ECU fine was imposed on 15 producers of polyprylene (ibid).

Thus, the Commission is seen to be doing something about collusion, and its actions have been generally applauded; nobody in

Europe argues that collusion between independent firms is a good thing which should be freely allowed. But the active pursuit of collusion only forms part of a coherent overall policy if there is an equally active and consistent prohibition of joint ventures which serve the same objectives as collusion. If the principle of consistent treatment for functionally equivalent arrangements is breached and joint ventures are allowed while collusion is penalised, then an active policy on collusion becomes merely a legal incitement to restructuring through joint venture. This is broadly what has happened in the EC.

The inconsistency in the treatment of collusion and joint ventures has one major cause: in cases of collusion, the maintenance of competition is virtually the sole consideration. Whereas, in cases of joint venture, balancing industrial policy considerations are given considerable weight. Article 85(3) is then used to provide a legal basis for the exemption of joint ventures which abridge competition. The industrial policy justification has been accepted not only in cases where joint venture promotes an important technical development but also in cases where companies are entering into defensive arrangements to cut capacity. Thus an Article 85(3) exemption was granted to a 'crisis cartel' of major synthetic fibre producers (including ICI, Rhone-Poulenc, Courtaulds and Hoechst AG) who proposed a common plan to reduce capacity to a set level; the firms entering into the agreement had a combined market share of over 50 per cent in all the products covered and roughly 75 per cent of the market in four of the products covered (CMLR, 1985, 1 at 789). In other cases where the Commission identifies a 'progressive' industrial policy justification, even larger abridgements of competition have been allowed. Thus, in a 1976 case involving German, French and British nuclear fuel re-processors, the Commission allowed capacity utilisation quotas and price fixing for oxide nuclear fuel re-processing in the three countries. The justification was that, in the absence of this agreement, the different states 'would rapidly take an incoherent set of decisions' to install (excess) capacity which they would then not be able to operate profitably; the argument was that this free-market outcome 'would certainly harm the Community's interests' (CMLR, 1976, 2 at D10).

The Commission avoids blatant contradiction by usually insisting that joint ventures should not explicitly enter into arrangements for price fixing and market sharing. Thus, in the case of the crisis cartel in synthetic fibres, the Commission insisted on the deletion

133

of clauses in the proposed agreement which specified production and delivery quotas. However, the difference between prohibiting production quotas and allowing capacity quotas is a fine one; in so far as capacity reductions bring industry supply into line with the current level of market demand, capacity quotas which the Commission allows would secure the same benefits for individual firms as production quotas which the Commission disallows. The fact is that the functional equivalence approach is not maintained; economically equivalent arrangements are judged according to the form adopted, and the lawyers who advise large corporations are sharp enough to spot the opportunity.

In some cases where a price fixing and market sharing cartel has been dissolved because it is illegal, some of the participants have turned to secure the same ends through a joint venture which has the Commission's blessing. For example, ICI and Enichem were both defendants in the PVC and polyethylene cartel case; the companies were fined 6 million and 6.5 million ECU respectively for playing a leading role in the cartel. In 1986 ICI and Enichem responded to the Commission's attack on the cartel by putting their PVC interests into a new joint venture, called European Vinyl Chloride, which is currently Europe's largest PVC producer (*Financial Times*, 22 December 1988). For the two participants, the new joint venture secures many of the objectives previously served by membership of the cartel; the form of the joint venture is such that the legally objectionable behaviour of price fixing and market sharing is unnecessary. Emboldened by this success, the chairman of Enimont (the new company formed by the merger of Enichem and Montedison Chemicals) has publicly hinted that a joint venture deal in polyethylene will be signed before the autumn of 1989 (*Financial Times*, 10 April 1989). As the Americans say, there is more than one way to skin a cat.

While alliance in joint venture form is largely unregulated, the control over mergers can be shown to be ineffectual. As we have seen, Article 86, for example, only states that 'any abuse by one or more undertakings of a dominant position within the Common Market or a substantial part of it shall be incompatible with the Common Market in so far as it may affect trade between member states'. The wording of Article 86 allows the Commission to regulate the 'abuse' of an existing 'dominant position' but makes it more difficult to regulate the creation or strengthening of a dominant position which would or could arise as the result of a merger.

However, the scope of Articles of the Treaty is determined by the way in which they are 'read', and decisions of the European Court play a key role in this respect. As far as Article 86 is concerned, the Court's interpretation of it in the *Continental Can* case of 1973 is an important landmark: in this case, the Court argued that Articles 85 and 86 had to be read in the light of Article 3(f) of the Treaty, 'whereby the activity of the Community includes the establishment of a system to protect competition within the Common Market from distortion' (CMLR, 1973, part 68 223). The Court went on to argue that, if Article 3(f) required that a system be established to prevent distortion of competition, then the same article required '*a fortiori*' that competition must not be 'eliminated'.

This judgement strengthened the Commission's hand, but it did not provide a basis for regulation of Euro-mergers. The 1973 judgement, for example, only applied to mergers which strengthened a dominant position; the creation of a dominant position was not covered. Some (e.g. Fine, 1987, p. 338) believe that the 1987 Phillip Morris case established the possibility that Article 85 could be applied to merger. If this view is correct, the Morris case is a major landmark because Article 85(3) would, as we have seen, then allow the introduction of balancing industrial policy criteria. Others (e.g. Korah and Lasok, 1988, p. 350) argue that the Morris case is not relevant to merger control, because the issue at stake was the acquisition of a minority interest.

While the Commission's position on joint ventures could be described as 'anything goes', its Article 86 policy on merger might be described as 'unlucky for some'. Under Article 86 only a small number of untypically dominant firms have to run the risk of a European prohibition on their merger activity. Intervention under Article 86 is only possible where merger raises issues about dominant power; unless there are special circumstances, dominance is practically interpreted as a 40 per cent plus share of one national market for a fairly narrow product range. It is hardly surprising that the classic EC merger cases concern untypical industries like tin cans and cigarettes, where production in the advanced countries is dominated by a handful of regional and international majors. Most European industries are very different. In motor cars, for example, there are 10 major producers, and only Fiat has, in EC terms, a dominant position in its national home market. In motor cars, a series of mergers which transformed the structure of the industry would, if Fiat was not involved, fall outside the EC's

Article 86 jurisdiction. In any event none of these industries – cans, cigarettes or cars – are typical in another important respect. The more frequent type of merger which will confront the Commission will be between enterprises operating in a variety of product markets, in which they have marked variations in market share, edge on competitors and so forth. On this kind of merger it is hardly too much to say that the Commission does not really have a policy.

In administrative terms also, Article 86 is an extraordinarily clumsy way of pursuing a few firms. Under Article 86, intervention is only straightforward after the combine has been formed; EC policy makers are then in the position of cooks trying to unscramble eggs. And as we have seen, prohibition is only possible on strict either/or criteria which relate to (abuse of) dominant position; under Article 86, no balancing industrial policy criteria can be invoked. The position on merger control under Article 86 is clearly unsatisfactory. The Commission has thus, over a long period, sought to gain agreement from the Council to a regulation on merger control. Negotiation has been difficult. In 1987 when the then Competition Commissioner, Peter Sutherland, wanted to obtain agreement on a new EC directive and regulation on merger, he threatened that, if national governments would not agree to the new measures, they would have to suffer the consequences of a strict, case-by-case enforcement of merger control under Articles 85 and 86. Agreement on the new merger regulation is likely some time in 1989, and the EC is now representing the new regulation as the solution to all the problems of merger control. But merger control is another case, like reform of the CAP, where critical examination suggests that the Commission's reach exceeds its grasp. The new regulation will give the Commission preemptive powers to inspect and rule on proposed mergers before they have been carried out. But that still means that the Commission has left many merger problems unresolved. The scope of the new regulation has yet to be settled, and it is not clear how the new criteria in the regulation will be applied.

The new regulation will cover more international mergers, but it is not yet clear how many more mergers will be covered. This is because there is still political argument about the turnover thresholds which should be applied. The EC originally proposed that mergers should fall within the Commission's ambit if the combined aggregate worldwide turnover of the firms involved was more than 1 billion ECU. The West German and British governments riposted by suggesting a 10 billion ECU threshold; at present levels of merger activity, that would mean domestic competition policy would apply in almost all instances (*Financial Times*, 9 January 1989). DG IV, the section of the Commission responsible for competition law, has a backlog of around 3,000 competition cases and is already, under existing legislation, acquiring some 100 new cases a year, which is slightly more than the number of cases which the Commission annually settles. Matters are further complicated because, under the new merger regulation, DG IV will, for the first time, have to meet strict deadlines about prompt decisions; Article 19(1) of the new regulation stipulates that mergers will be deemed to be authorised if the Commission has not arrived at a decision within four months.

Even more fundamentally, the new merger regulation does not resolve the old confusions about which criteria should be applied to restructuring and how the claims of competition and industrial policy should be balanced in merger control. These confusions are not so much resolved as reinscribed in the new regulation. The confusion is compounded because formally the new regulation 'implements rather than supersedes Article 86'. The most recent draft uses the term 'concentrations' rather than 'mergers' and states that they 'shall not be compatible with the Common Market when they give rise to or strengthen a dominant position in the Common Market or a substantial part thereof'. This closes one loophole, by allowing the Commission to rule on mergers which create a dominant position, but it is not clear that such mergers will usually be prohibited. This is because Article 2(4) confirms the exceptions embodied in Article 85(3): 'The Commission shall authorise concentrations as compatible with the Common Market where they contribute to the attainment of basic objectives of the Treaty . . .' Essentially, the new regulation introduces explicit balancing industrial policy criteria that are notably absent from Article 86, which has hitherto been used for merger control; the new regulation appears to be modelled on the form of Article 85, where 85(3) introduces the balancing criteria. Thus Article 2(4) of the draft regulation goes on to state that merger is acceptable provided it contributes 'to improving production and distribution, to promoting technical or economic progress or to improving the competitive structure of the common market, taking due account of the competitiveness of the undertakings concerned with regard to international competition and of the interests of consumers . . .'

Everything depends on how this industrial policy justification is interpreted and applied by the Commission and the European Court. Precedent suggests that Article 2(4) may be used to license a very liberal regime where few mergers are prohibited; after all, in the decisions on joint venture, the industrial policy justification under Article 85(3) has been almost invariably accepted as valid.

This suspicion is confirmed by the public statements of senior politicians in Brussels. They emphasise that the intention is to make merger generally easier rather than selectively more difficult. Thus Commissioner Sutherland in the European Parliament (16 November 1987) claimed that the 'sole aim' of the new measures was to remove legal obstacles to cross-border merger. It is equally significant that the French government has recently changed sides on the issue of the new regulation. For much of the 1970s and the 1980s, the French government aligned with the West Germans and the British to block the introduction of a new directive and regulation of mergers. If the French have now changed sides, it is because they support the industrial policy justification and believe that the new regulation will give EC companies valuable help in overcoming national objections to cross-border takeover. Madame Cresson, the French Trade Minister, apparently believes that the new European regulation is a way of neutralising the Bundeskartellamt (*Financial Times*, 22 December 1988). On this view, the logical next step would be an attack on the defensive blocks which, under German and Dutch law, can be used to make companies bid-proof. The EC has already moved to outlaw the defensive tactics which Société Générale of Belgium used successfully against Benedetti; under new EC rules, it will be illegal to dilute the value of a hostile bidder's holding by making a special capital issue after a hostile bid has been announced (*Financial Times*, 23 December 1988).

All in all, the new merger regulation is not going to emerge as a tough, effective way of controlling mergers; it is more likely to become a new licence to merge for Euro-nationals who are already free to enter into joint venture. The Commission has promised a Europe without frontiers. For ordinary citizens the frontier controls will remain, but for big business some of the frontier controls are being abolished. Europe will be a newly discovered continent of opportunity for Benedetti, Maxwell and Hahn. When their press releases announce bold new alliances, 1992 will figure as an all-purpose rationalisation; every merger and joint venture will be publicly justified as 'necessary to meet the challenge of 1992'. This is nicely ironic. In the late 1980s, 1992 was originally sold to Europe as a politically controlled real instrument for increasing competition; now it is going to be repackaged for popular consumption in the early 1990s as a businessman's excuse for the uncontrolled abridgement of competition. In a kind of after life, 1992 will serve as a fig leaf for European big business.

Chapter 5
What Next?

In this book we have sought to analyse the broad economic and political issues relevant to the internal market programme. We have pointed out that, for the Commission, the programme was a means of facilitating the integration of the European Community and that this distinguished it from a pure liberal market economic initiative. In terms of this political objective, there is no doubt that the programme has proved a major success. But the outcome is not so much a triumph as a struggle, and our book so far has illustrated several aspects of the struggle for Europe. There is a discursive struggle to impose an economic problem definition; the consequences of unbalanced trade flows and centralisation of production have been ignored so that the economics debate can be concentrated upon the benefits of trade. This takes place against the background of a political struggle to impose a liberal market definition on developing European institutions; the 1992 programme has been used as a lever to achieve integration while liberal collectivists and socialists have been bought off with false promises of compensation through social and regional policy. While outside, in the real world, which escapes the categories of liberal market economic and political discourse, big business manoeuvres for advantage, German manufacturers continue their export drive, and in the run-up to the single market, big business seeks advantage through mergers and joint ventures. In this final chapter, we turn to examine the next phase of the struggle: what comes after 1992 when the single market is (symbolically) completed?

The question of whether the single market will bring forth its bounties will continue to be debated by economists. But the politicians have already moved on to dispute and plan what might come next. This development was particularly striking in Britain where politicians were initially slow to understand the significance and implications of the 1992 programme. In Britain the debate on 1992 only got under way in Spring 1988 when the Cecchini Report was published; just six months later in September 1988, Prime Minister Thatcher and the Labour Opposition leader, Neil Kinnock, were making major speeches about what (if anything) should follow the completion of the 1992 programme. The old British question of the 1970s, articulated in the Wilson referendum, was: 'Are we for or against the EC?' At the end of the 1980s, after a long period of silence, a new kind of question was articulated: 'What kind of Europe do we want to be members of?' In the first two sections of this chapter we consider the different answers of Thatcher and Kinnock to this question.

While British politicians have been prophesying and predicting the Euro-future, the Brussels politicians have been planning it. From the Commission's point of view, it is crucial that the impetus to unification generated by the 1992 programme should not be dissipated and lost. The Commission's question, as always, is: 'How can the cause of European unification be advanced?' Their new answer involves a process of monetary unification which would irrevocably lock the different economies together. Monetary unification had originally been proposed in the early 1970s, when it came to nothing; the Exchange Rate Mechanism (ERM), which ties the value of eight Community currencies together, is the only enduring result of this earlier initiative. Emboldened by the success of the 1992 programme, the Commission is now trying again. The EC summit at Hanover in June 1988 set up a committee on monetary unification chaired by Jacques Delors. In its report of April 1989, the Delors Committee made detailed proposals for monetary unification. In the last two sections of this chapter, we consider the character and significance of this official programme for the next phase, before finally turning to consider how liberal collectivists and socialists should respond to this new initiative.

A corporatist, collectivist Europe?

The spectre of a corporatist, collectivist Europe now haunts the British right. It is a spectre which was conjured up in one speech by the Prime Minister at Bruges in September 1988; her intellectual fellow travellers, like Lord Harris and Professor Minogue, took their lead from the lady when they called their newly-formed European pressure group 'the Bruges group'. Mrs Thatcher's influence over these gurus of the right is sustained by her (inflated) sense of historic mission and her (self-deluding) capacity to identify turning points and achievements. These qualities were well to the fore in the Bruges speech, in which Mrs Thatcher warned that the British revolution was now threatened by new European developments which it was her duty to resist; 'we have not successfully rolled back the frontiers of the State in Britain, only to see them re-imposed at a European level, with a European Superstate exercising a new dominance' (Thatcher, 1988, p. 4). This development was both threatening and futile because it ignored 'the lesson of the economic history of Europe in the 1970s and 1980s'; in her view, this lesson was simply that a 'state-controlled economy is a recipe for low growth, and . . . free enterprise within a framework of law brings better results' (Thatcher, 1988, p. 6).

Mrs Thatcher's position on European economic integration is determined by her commitment to deregulation. For her, freedom in Europe (as elsewhere) means freedom from regulation; 'our aim should not be more and detailed regulation from the centre, it should be to deregulate and to remove the constraints on trade' (Thatcher, 1988, p. 6). Thus, she applauded the 1992 programme because it involved 'getting rid of barriers'. Even if Jacques Delors was not one of us, his 1992 programme was an exemplary attempt to make Europe like Mrs Thatcher's Britain; 'the aim of a Europe open to enterprise is the motive force behind the creation of the Single European Act' (Thatcher, 1988, p. 6). Mrs Thatcher read – and acted on – the economic text of the 1992 programme; the political sub-text was ignored. Thus, in 1987 her government did not protest or refuse to sign the Single European Act, which significantly reduced her ability to block further development of the EC. But after the Delors Committee on monetary unification was set up in the summer of 1988, it was no longer possible to ignore the fact that the EC planned a next phase which was, in Thatcherite terms, regulationist. At Bruges, it was Delors' turn to be handbagged. Mrs Thatcher insisted that she believed in the free movement of capital, a free market in financial services and greater use of the ECU, but she was firmly opposed to the creation of a European central bank formulating a unified European monetary policy. Her position subsequently formed the basis of Nigel Lawson's response as Chancellor of the Exchequer to the Delors Committee report in April 1989. Their differences over monetary policy encouraged Mrs Thatcher's suspicions about what Brussels might intend in other policy areas: 'If we are to have a European Company Statute, it should contain the minimum regulations. And certainly we in Britain would fight attempts to introduce collectivism and corporatism at the European level' (Thatcher, 1988, p. 7).

In opposing corporatist Europe, Mrs Thatcher is fighting imaginary dragons. Whatever Brussels intends, the Commission does not plan to create a corporatist state of institutions and processes where organised labour is a major partner with big business and government. In this respect, the official literature on 1992 adequately conveys a message which has not changed. In the 1985 White Paper and the Cecchini Report, organised labour had no visible economic or political role. Apart from the European Community institutions of Council, Commission and Parliament, the major actors were governments, business and consumers, who would all benefit from increased competition. There was no discussion of whether these processes might harm the interests of organised labour or how trade unions might be represented or safeguarded. Such concessions are politically unnecessary because European trade unions are now in a very weak position to press for, and take, more than the Commission gives. Unions in most of Europe have declined in number, and even more in influence, during the 1980s. In France, Spain and Portugal less than one-third of the labour force is organised, and in previously strong areas like the Netherlands, union membership has fallen to about one-third. What the Commission does offer European labour are some health and safety standards and, maybe, the prospect of German-style worker participation in enterprise management. This is not, of course, the same thing as a corporatist role in the institutions of supra-national government. And as we shall argue in the next section, the Commission's failure to secure the adoption of modest directives on participation or health and safety shows that the balance of political forces inside the EC is against labour.

While corporatist Europe is not on the agenda, collectivist Europe is a possibility created by the confusions of Mrs Thatcher. The Bruges speech did not identify the preconditions of a liberal market Europe and naively equated regulation and institutions with collectivism. According to Mrs Thatcher, removing NTBs is a worthwhile liberal market project, but locking the currencies and building a European bank is an unnecessary collectivist project. This distinction is unsustainable. A single market in manufactured goods cannot exist if national currencies are appreciating and depreciating. The single market logically requires a tight monetary alliance or monetary union which would have to be managed in some way by new supra-national institutions. It is (just) possible to conceive of a project of national deregulation which involved the liberalisation of existing economic regulations within a framework of national institutions and regulations. In this case, the main thrust of liberal market policy could be to abolish or simplify existing regulations and institutions. But the European project is a project of international integration which involves the sponsoring of new economic relations. Here, it is essential to have new kinds of regulation and institutions to manage what has not existed before. At the European level, the liberal market solution, just like the liberal collectivist or socialist solution, depends on new kinds of regulations and institutions. The political issue is not whether to regulate, but what form the regulations and institutions should take.

If Mrs Thatcher is opposed to European regulation, that is because new European regulations and institutions limit national 'sovereignty'; as she insisted in the Bruges speech, 'willing and active co-operation between independent sovereign states is the best way to build a successful European Community' (Thatcher, 1988, p. 4). Ultimately, it is not liberal market economics but political nationalism which determines her position on Europe. For Mrs Thatcher, the nation state provides an economic space for the expression of irreducible cultural differences: 'Europe will be stronger precisely because it has France as France, Spain as Spain, Britain as Britain, each with its own customs, traditions and identity' (Thatcher, 1988, p. 4). The cultural differences are such that each nation should be free to make its own choice between market individualism and collectivism: 'we in Britain would fight attempts to introduce collectivism and corporatism at the European level – although what people want to do in their own countries is a matter for them' (Thatcher, 1988, p. 7). Whether self-consciously or not, much of what Mrs Thatcher has to say about 'nationhood' vaguely echoes de Gaulle's old theme of '*Europe des Patries*'. What has been little registered in Britain is the point that there is a large gap between de Gaulle's statesmanship and Mrs Thatcher's posturing (for an exception see *Financial Times*, 27 September 1988).

Nationhood is itself a slippery and dangerous concept. On all the available evidence, Scotland rejects Mrs Thatcher's liberal market policies. But presumably that does not count because, for Mrs Thatcher, the Scots (like the Irish) are not a nation. De Gaulle took a broader and more realistic view of nationality, as his positions on Quebec and Algeria clearly demonstrate. Furthermore, Mrs Thatcher's position on existing sovereign states is painfully inconsistent. De Gaulle's preference for national sovereignty was more uniformly expressed in the form of resolute hostility to any politics of power blocs and alliances; French troops were, for example, removed from the NATO command structure. But Mrs Thatcher, the scourge of the EC, is also, paradoxically, the staunch defender of NATO; in economic policy it is wrong to cede sovereign power to the supra-national EC, whereas in defence policy it is right to cede sovereign power to the supra-national NATO. If Mrs Thatcher's vision is more inconsistent than de Gaulle's, it also fails the test of statesmanship; Thatcher's vision is not harnessed to any realisable purpose. *Europe des Patries* served the old French purpose of keeping Britain out. Nationhood can hardly serve the new British purpose of moulding Europe now that Britain is irrevocably in. Thatcher's position on Europe's supra-national institutions and regulations is blankly negative because she wishes to retain national sovereignty. At the same time, she does not envisage sovereignty being used for any positive economic purpose; sovereignty is that which allows the British people to express their newly-discovered hostility to collectivism by voting again for Mrs Thatcher. It is not surprising that this chauvinist and egocentric vision of nationality finds no allies on the European mainland. As the French Prime Minister, Michel Rocard, observed, Mrs Thatcher proposes Europe as 'a plane without a pilot'. Without mainland allies, Mrs Thatcher is Don(na) Quixote tilting at European collectivism. Before and after she retires to Dulwich, the outcome of the struggle for Europe will be decided by other forces.

Social Europe?

After ten years of Tory rule, the British Labour party's hostility to Europe has turned into enthusiasm. Labour now wants to join the forces moulding the new Europe, partly because many senior Labour politicians and trade unionists see Europe as an opportunity to obtain at a supra-national level some of the things which Mrs.

Thatcher has prevented them from getting in Britain (see, for example, Willis, *New Statesman*, 19 August 1988). They were powerfully reinforced in this belief by Jacques Delors' speech to the British TUC in autumn 1988; not only did the President of the Commission speak of 'social Europe', he also spent more time with British trade unionists in twenty-four hours than Mrs Thatcher had done in the previous decade.

The Labour vision of Europe was articulated by Neil Kinnock in a significant speech of September 1988 in Glasgow, where he addressed the socialist group of the European Parliament. Like Mrs Thatcher, Neil Kinnock starts from a reading of history, though the lesson which he draws is, of course, less concise and quite different.

> Every one of our [labour] movements in every one of our countries has, by a variety of means . . . made constant efforts to civilise the operation of markets and to make economic activity compatible with human security. In some respects, the relative comfort and safety of modern life is due to the success achieved by socialists and others who realise that life is too important to be left to the dictates of demand and supply. That is the spirit in which we must approach the new scale of market operation. (Kinnock, 1988, p. 3)

Thus Mr Kinnock begins by challenging the assumption 'that the [single market] will exclusively and inevitably be an open space for the operation of New Right economics' (Kinnock, 1988, p. 2). That outcome is not inevitable, because Europe is a new sphere in which the labour movement can realise its historic mission of accepting and civilising the market.

The 1992 programme is cautiously accepted in the Glasgow speech: the single-market programme contains 'sensible measures' for the removal of NTBs, and this liberalisation will bring 'economic opportunity'. But, Mr Kinnock argues that the economic benefits of 1992 have been exaggerated and liberal market economics ignores the social costs. If 'market power' has complete economic and political dominance in western Europe, that will have unacceptable consequences for 'civil rights and environmental conditions, individual opportunities and collective provisions' (Kinnock, 1988, p. 3). Even in narrow economic terms, the market is a mixed blessing because it will lead 'to the reinforcement of existing imbalances in the European economy, concentrating industry, employment and prosperity in those parts of Europe that are already strongest' (Kinnock, 1988, p. 5). And while the promise of 1992 is increased competition, the likely outcome will be monopolistic and oligopolistic control by big business. According to Mr Kinnock, 'social Europe' is the appropriate civilising response; 1992 must be accompanied by a balancing programme of measures which redress the consequences of the market. Social Europe offers 'productive and socially just solutions' which secure the ultimate objective of 'the enhancement of the quality of life of all the peoples of Europe' (Kinnock, 1988, p. 6).

Most people would find it difficult to disagree with this laudable objective which is shared by all men and women of goodwill. Which perhaps just means that the authors of this book would not disagree with the general thrust of Mr Kinnock's analysis of the consequences of the market; our earlier chapters illustrate and develop many of the points about the market which Mr Kinnock makes in summary form. But finding a phrase is not the same thing as solving a problem, and we would question whether 'social Europe' is an economically adequate and politically practicable response to the combined threat posed by liberal market economics and European big business. A first set of questions concerns the content of the social Europe programme: does the programme contain policy instruments which are adequate to the problems which have been diagnosed? And a second set of questions concerns its political practicability: is the balance of political forces in the Community such that socialists and liberal collectivists can secure a 'widely and effectively applied' programme? If the instruments are inadequate and the political balance is unfavourable, then Mr Kinnock becomes a pilot without a plane.

At one point in the Glasgow speech, Mr Kinnock argues that 'a whole range of complementary policies need to be put in place to make . . . [the single market] work for the peoples of the Community' (Kinnock, 1988, pp. 3–4). In a later speech, he spoke more cautiously about the need for 'a social agenda' (Kinnock, 1989, p. 2). On closer inspection, social Europe turns out to be an agenda rather than a set of policy instruments. In his Glasgow speech, Mr Kinnock identified some of the problems to be addressed; these included the migration of industry, employment and prosperity to the centre of Europe and the abridgement of competition through mergers and take-overs. He also provided a list of desiderata; the desirable outcomes included co-ordinated European reflation, expansion with balanced trade, upward harmonisation in workers' rights and conditions of work, and economic democracy which would ensure that enterprises are accountable to customers and communities as well as to employees. There was no recognition that some of these objectives could only be achieved at the expense of others, nor was there any detailed specification of policy instruments which would be adequate to secure any of these objectives. Mr Kinnock's attempt to address the issues of trade imbalance and centralisation of production only reinforces our doubts about the credibility of social Europe.

Mr Kinnock believes it is necessary to address the unevenness of development and to redress the disadvantage of the periphery; it is essential to ensure 'the acceptance of the principle and practice of government or EC intervention for the purpose of ensuring development in regions that do not have advantages of location in the central area of the single market' (Kinnock, 1988, p. 7). Such intervention could take two forms: a primary policy on the location of industry could be used to block expansion at the centre or induce expansion at the periphery; alternatively, a secondary policy of redistribution could be used to transfer income or increase the attractions of the periphery without interfering with market mechanisms. Mr Kinnock seems to prefer the latter type of intervention since he endorses existing EC regional and social policy with the caveat that 'the social and regional funds must be substantial enough to offer support to those parts of the Community which will most feel the disruptive effects of the new market arrangements' (Kinnock, 1988, p. 6). The presumption seems to be that the implementation of the existing proposals to reform the structural funds and double their size will be enough to 'promote regional development and to correct regional imbalance'.

It is a prescription which lacks credibility. Mr Kinnock vastly overestimates the scale and efficacy of EC regional and social expenditure, and worse still, in common with many on the European left, he misrecognises the (liberal market) character of the intervention. As we argued in Chapter Three, even if the social and regional funds are enlarged, they will still represent modest expenditures; if the funds are doubled in real terms by 1992, they will still account for less than one-half of 1 per cent of Community GDP. Furthermore, expenditure from the funds is concentrated on liberal market objects (training and improvement of infrastructure), while the iniquitous matching grant system seeks to redirect national government expenditure onto these reactionary objects. The question is not whether all this amounts to an adequate progressive intervention, but why it is (mis)read as a progressive intervention. In our view, Mr Kinnock's bias toward secondary redistribution is naturally generated by a social democratic revisionism which identifies socialism simply as the market plus add-on redistribution.

In Mr Kinnock's speech, socialist revisionism has the same fundamental status as nationalism in the Bruges speech; it is the unexamined premise on which the notion of appropriate policy is founded. Of course, social policy does matter and is important in its own right, but there is no evidence that it can bear the exaggerated load which revisionism puts upon it. Certainly, it is irresponsible to presume that it can bear this load until adequate instruments of redistribution are specified. Until that is done, our presumption would be that the regressive effects associated with trade and market integration can only be dealt with by challenging the economic mechanisms of the market.

Labour's domestic and European policies share the same revisionist content; the only difference is that Labour's domestic political strategy has long been conditioned by unnecessary defeatism, but on Europe, Labour's optimism knows no bounds. Partly, this is because Mr Kinnock knows that, in Europe, he is not, like Mrs Thatcher, in a minority of one. The call for social Europe has been taken up by virtually all the major figures on the European left. In 1988, the French Prime Minister, Michel Rocard, was said to be 'firmly committed to the principles of the free market, tempered by the claims of social justice' (*Financial Times*, 24 October 1988). The Greek President of the European Council, Mr Papoulias, in his initial address to the Parliament in July 1988 joined the chorus when he stressed the need to press towards 'the single social area' (*Bulletin of the EC*, 1988, no. 7/8, p. 169). In these circumstances it was easy for the British Labour leader to convince himself that, if he was not in a majority, he was (for once) on the side that was winning. It is understandable in these circumstances that Mr Kinnock, like other senior Labour figures, has not examined too closely what is on offer and what the Commission can deliver in the area of the social.

The Commission has no official plans for introducing any of the ambitious proposals which figure in unofficial 'social Europe' visions; the levelling-up of social security or the establishment of minimum wages, for example, are not on the Commission's agenda. The Commission is, instead, sponsoring modest initiatives in the areas of worker participation and health and safety. Under the proposed Fifth Directive, workers in companies which employ more than 1,000 persons would be offered a separate management or places on the (main) supervisory board. Worker representatives would have a right to consultation on some important issues such as factory closure and alliances with other firms. But workers would not be able to veto decisions or to obtain third-party arbitration; under the provisions of Article 4, a separate management board would have no powers of decision, and workers who sit on the (main) supervisory board will be in a permanent minority. This kind of worker participation may encourage good industrial relations practice, but it will not allow workers to fight the effects of industrial restructuring. On health and safety, in May 1988 the Commission published a new framework directive with five associated 'daughter' directives covering the areas of minimum workplace standards, machinery safety, visual display units, heavy loads and personal protective equipment (*Industrial Relations Review and Report*, 5 July 1988). These initiatives are to be welcomed, but those who read the directives will find that they offer worker protection coloured by general deregulationist and liberal market conceptions; the directives recognise the need to 'avoid imposing administrative, financial and legal constraints which would hold back the creation and development of small and medium-sized undertakings'. Paradoxically, safety regulation is to be eased for those smaller firms which research shows usually have higher accident rates (on British construction, for example, see Dawson et al., 1988, p. 126).

The proposed measures on worker participation and health and safety would not greatly reduce the privileges of capitalist owners and managers. For that reason, they should be relatively uncontroversial. The necessity for worker participation and health and safety legislation is already accepted at a national level by several right-of-centre European governments; Chancellor Kohl's Christian Democrats are firmly committed to maintaining the works' council system of representation, which has survived every change of government since the Weimar republic. Thus, in our view, the progress of the Commission's proposals on participation and safety is a crucial test of the balance between progressive and reactionary forces in the struggle for social Europe. If progress cannot be made on these two initiatives, a more ambitious social Europe programme looks to be a non-starter.

The Fifth Directive, on worker participation, was originally tabled in 1972, and it has still not been adopted. Partly, this is because the measure raised issues about levelling down in countries with worker participation, as well as issues about levelling up in countries without worker representation. But increasingly, the problem is that one member government and many employer groups are implacably opposed. The Commission offered a revised draft directive on worker participation at the Hanover summit in May 1988. Despite attempts to placate the British government, British opposition was reaffirmed, and that may now be a road-block; worker representation is an issue which probably still requires unanimity in the Council of Ministers. Employers' organis-ations have also been active in opposing EC-wide regulation of worker participation. For example, the Round Table of European Industrialists, a pressure group which represents Europe's 40 largest multinationals, wrote to the 12 EC governments urging that mem-ber states should be free to set their own systems of worker participation (*Financial Times*, 11 November 1988). Health and safety proposals have failed to progress for much the same reasons. The British government viewed the May 1988 proposals as un-necessary Euro-regulation. Lord Young, the then British Trade Secretary, insisted that the British government would not agree to

> placing unnecessary burdens and regulations on employers. These can only increase costs and damage employment . . . It is from this basis that we shall look at any proposals from the commission to introduce new forms of legislation or to impose industrial relations which would turn the clock back to the 1970s. (*Financial Times*, 27 October 1988)

UNICE, the main European employers' federation, accepted the principle of EC social action limited to health and safety, training and worker mobility. But at the same time, UNICE argued that the first task was to complete the internal market and refused negotiations with the European TUC; UNICE is only prepared to enter into discussions on health and safety with the ETUC (*Financial Times*, 10 January 1989).

In terms of both worker representation and health and safety, a change of government in Britain would help to remove the block-age. But that would hardly guarantee success when business pres-sure groups remain hostile and the Commission is not now pressing hard for substantial progress on either worker representation or health and safety.

The plan for monetary union

The nature of the European constitution is such that the Commission and its two-term President, Jacques Delors, have considerable powers of political initiative. The powers of the European Parliament are still severely limited; it may become, but is not yet, a legislature like the British Parliament. The European Parliament only has a right to consultation about legislation and a limited power to disrupt by refusing to vote expenditure. The Council of Ministers provides the framework for the formal participation of the governments of the member states. Traditionally, the Council has had considerable power to block legislation because each member state has a veto in the Council of Ministers; the Single European Act of 1987 for the first time introduced qualified majority voting in the Council. But the power of initiative does not lie with the Council, which only adopts the principal legal acts after they have been proposed by the Commission. The Commission, which is not elected but nominated by the national governments, is the body which proposes specific legislation.

It was the Commission which initiated and pressed for the single market programme. By 1988, the question was how to follow up this success. The single market programme had generated considerable momentum but only slow progress had been made on a range of outstanding issues like tax harmonisation, which divided the EC members. There was also the risk of disillusionment and cynicism as it became increasingly clear that 'Europe without frontiers' and a single market in financial services would not materialise. Initially, in 1988, it seemed as though the Commission was pursuing a two-track policy for monetary union and social Europe in the next phase after 1992. By Spring 1989, it was clear that monetary union was the overriding priority. This tactical choice may seem curious when Delors is a former French socialist Minister of Finance; surely Delors would prefer to be remembered after 1992 as the statesman who introduced progressive social policies, rather than as the hatchetman who enforced orthodox banking notions of sound finance? In our view, the tactical switch provides one more illustration of the point that, for many who are socialists, the transcendent political aim is building Europe; the means are judged pragmatically, according to their effectiveness in realising that end.

Monetary union is a long-standing enthusiasm of the President.

Before his initial appointment in 1985, Delors apparently considered making monetary union the main goal. But he was persuaded that monetary union was then impracticable because it raised the issue of sovereignty too directly. The removal of NTBs was more acceptable to member states, so Delors opted for the Cockfield plan for a single market. This 1992 programme postponed rather than displaced the project of monetary union. The official literature on 1992 repeatedly presents monetary union or tight monetary alliance as the inevitable and logical solution to problems about exchange rate stability, which would arise when capital movements were liberalised. Thus Cecchini wrote,

> a European home market is likely to increase exchange rate fluctuations: intensification of intra-EC trade and liberalisation of transborder capital movements – indispensable as they are for achieving the gains of market integration – may well heighten monetary instability. Success in creating the internal market thus condemns the Community to strengthen the European monetary system and build the institutional framework needed to guarantee intra-EC exchange rate stability. (Cecchini, 1988, p. 106)

Much the same line was taken in the Padoa-Schioppa report, a Commission-sponsored study on the strategy of implementing the single market. One of the four central propositions of the strategy group was that 'monetary policy co-ordination and the mechanisms of the European Monetary System (EMS) will have to be significantly strengthened if freedom of capital movements and exchange rate discipline are to survive and co-exist'. This was seen as a minimalist necessity, although from an economic point of view full 'monetary union is the first-best solution' (Padoa-Schioppa, 1987, pp. x and 83).

Nevertheless, in the summer and autumn of 1988, Delors stumped Europe to call for a 'social dimension' to the single market. His speeches, such as the one to the British TUC, sounded considerably more radical than they were. Delors made no mention of minimum wage legislation or levelling up of social service provisions. Social Europe was largely identified with the Commission's proposals for health and safety regulation and worker participation which had been watered down in 1988 in the hope of improving their acceptability. The limited scope of these proposals was more accurately indicated in a Delors address to the European Parliament in January 1987 when he spoke of the beginnings of a

European 'social area' (Delors, 1987). The public emphasis on social Europe served a number of purposes: it reassured labour that 1992 did not mean a businessman's Europe; it kept the blocked directives on worker representation and health and safety on the agenda; and it (indirectly) rebuked the British government which, in Delors' view, had a passion for exaggerated deregulation (*Financial Times*, 24 September 1988). No doubt, Delors was sincere when he insisted that 'economic success and social cohesion were inextricably mixed' (*Financial Times*, 14 September 1988). What he did not say was that social cohesion was being postponed so that monetary union could be pressed more effectively.

The monetary objectives came out of the closet at the Hanover summit in mid-1988. Delors successfully pressed for the establishment of a high-level monetary study group. This Committee, chaired by Delors himself, was to report in 1989 on possibilities for improving monetary cooperation. Two separate post-midnight press briefings were given, one by the Commission President and one by the West German Chancellor. At these the mood was described as 'euphoric', and the path towards monetary union was presented in 'almost visionary terms' (*Financial Times*, 29 June 1988). The personal identification of Delors with the project of monetary unification was underlined when, in autumn 1988, Delors did not allocate responsibility for monetary affairs to any of the newly-appointed commissioners; the President kept this portfolio for himself. Progress on the monetary front was assured by the way in which the Delors Committee was packed with central bank governors who shared the values of financial orthodoxy; ministers and civil servants representing national governments were effectively excluded. After considerable effort, the Delors Committee presented a unanimous report on monetary unification in April 1989, and this report will be considered at EC summits in Madrid and Paris later in 1989.

In 1989, monetary union is no longer the object that dare not speak its name. The Delors Committee plans 'the elimination of margins of fluctuation and the irrevocable locking of exchange rate parities', with the adoption of a single Community currency following in due course as 'a natural and further development of the monetary union'. Loss of sovereignty is boldly confronted as an inescapable consequence of the new union: 'the permanent fixing of exchange rates would deprive individual countries of an important instrument for the correction of economic imbalance and for independent action in the pursuit of national objectives, especially price stability.' These assaults on national economic autonomy are sweetened by the obligatory reference to the need for 'more effective structural and regional policies' to deal with any problems that arise: 'the reform of the structural funds and doubling of their resources would be fully implemented to ensure the ability of Community policies to promote regional development and to correct economic imbalances'. But this reference to regional and social policy is as gestural as the similar reference in the 1985 *White Paper*, which planned the single market. Almost the whole text of the Delors Report is concerned with the plan for a three-stage progression to full monetary union.

The Report is effectively a timetable without a calendar; the Delors Committee believes it is not possible to foresee when conditions will allow progress to the later stages. But the process of union should begin on a definite date in the near future; Stage One is to begin on 1 July 1990. This first stage involves the transformation of the existing Exchange Rate Mechanism (ERM), which is a loose monetary alliance that includes only eight of the twelve EC currencies. On 1 July 1990 all twelve national currencies are to be brought within the ERM, which will subsequently operate as a tight(er) monetary alliance. The rates of exchange between the different currencies will not be immutably fixed, and this will allow the weaker countries to secure some relief from competitive pressures through small devaluations. But in principle, 'other means of adjustment are to be preferred', and it is also suggested 'that the same rules would apply to all the participants in the ERM'. Stage One inaugurates a new regime of regulation which will be operated through existing institutions. No new monetary institutions are created at this stage, but the already extant committee of central bank governors will be able to put forward proposals on monetary and macro-economic policy to the Council of Ministers.

At Stage Two the institutions necessary for monetary unification will be put into place. This will lead to 'collective decision making' although 'ultimate responsibility for policy decisions will remain at this stage with national authorities'. This responsibility is likely to be more nominal than real because at this stage the new institutions will establish a comprehensive system of tutelage over national monetary and fiscal policy. At Stage Two, a new institution, the European System of Central Banks (ESCB), is to be set up; it will take 'centralised and collective decisions . . . on the supply of money and credit as well as on other instruments of monetary policy, including interest rates'. Thus, the ESCB will formulate the 'general thrust of monetary policy' and cooperate with the Council of Economic and Finance Ministers in determining exchange rate policy. With respect to the project of monetary union, it was only to be expected that the Delors Committee would propose some kind of European central bank. Less predictable, and more striking, is the proposal to bring national fiscal policy into the Stage Two system of tutelage. While the ESCB supervises monetary policy, the Council of Ministers will supervise fiscal policy. The Council of Ministers will lay down 'precise – although not yet binding – rules relating to the size of annual budget deficits and their financing'.

Stage Two is intended as 'a period of transition to the final stage'. With the new institutional system of tutelage in place, the regulations which limit and prevent devaluation can be tightened. At Stage Two, any realignment of national exchange rates is meant to be a measure of last resort, and the ESCB, with the Council of Ministers, will have the power to enforce adjustment by other means. Thus it is possible for the Delors Committee to envisage a third stage, in which the exchange rates between national currencies are to be 'irrevocably locked' while the preferred solution of a single European currency is reached. At this final stage the institutional constraints will be tightened. For example, the ESCB will acquire and manage all currency reserves and decide on exchange market intervention in third currencies, while the Council will impose binding rules on budget deficits and the ways in which they are financed.

The Delors Committee Report of 1989 is different from the single market *White Paper* of 1985 because it boldly confronts, and plans, the curtailment of national autonomy. But the old procedural skills which were partly responsible for the success of the earlier initiative are being applied to the new initiative. The principle of taking the low ground first – and quickly – has again clearly been applied; Stage One, which involves a much tighter monetary alliance, begins in mid–summer 1990. There is also a renewed insistence that member states must accept the whole package. Not only does the Commission try to block clause-by-clause negotiation before the event, it also now proposes to block recrimination and renegotiation after the event: 'the decision to enter upon the first stage should be a decision to embark on the entire process.' And for those countries which may suspect that tutelage means bondage, the Commission makes the option of staying out as unattractive as possible. The new arrangements will be run on a collective 'club' basis, and those who stay outside the club will lose any chance to influence the rules of the club; 'pending the full participation of all member states – which is of prime importance – influence on the management of each set of arrangements would have to be related to the degree of participation by member states.'

The plan for monetary union opens a new phase in the struggle for Europe. Its publication raises two questions: how much of the plan will be implemented, and what does it signify? The answers to the two questions are interrelated because how much happens will depend on how the member states read the intentions and consequences of the Delors plan for monetary union.

It can be said that we have been here before; the Werner report in 1970 called for the establishment of European monetary union within a decade but led to nothing except the ERM, which was set up at the very end of that decade. But the present proposals are much more fully specified and carry the weight of unanimity amongst the governors of the national central banks. The initial response of the different national governments was encouraging, from the Commission's point of view. Only the British government immediately rejected the plan, because it disapproved of the whole project; Chancellor Lawson claimed that the plan would 'require political union, a united states of Europe, which is not on the agenda' (*Financial Times*, 19 April 1989). But the reactions of other governments suggest that monetary union is on the agenda, although there are substantial differences of opinion about how quickly monetary union could and should be achieved. On monetary union, commentators discerned a broad division between the so-called pragmatists (West Germany, Britain and Luxemburg) and the enthusiasts (France, Spain and Italy). The first group considered that the recommendations would only be implemented in the distant future; the latter group were impatient for rapid progress. There is no sign of a broad 'coalition of the disadvantaged', but the Delors plan could be modified or shelved at either of the 1989 EC summits in Madrid and Paris. The decisive battles may be postponed until the Commission presses for a definite date for transition to Stage Two; the creation of the ESCB at Stage Two requires changes in the EC treaties and would presumably have to be unanimously approved by all member countries. The Commission's tactics will almost certainly be to press for an early start on Stage One with agreement 'in principle' to go further.

It is paradoxical that France, Italy and Spain are classed among the enthusiasts who wish to push towards monetary union, because the Delors plan proposes a system of tutelage which is likely to constrain their room for manoeuvre. With devaluation increasingly blocked, the payments deficits of the less competitive countries will have to be resolved by deflationary domestic monetary and fiscal policies; in Stages Two and Three, the EC will be able to enforce such a policy. Acceptance of such a plan is a real *volte-face* for Italy, which is now backing a regime of fixed exchange rates. Italy only agreed to enter the ERM of the European Monetary System on condition that the lire would be allowed to fluctuate within a currency parity band of plus or minus 6 per cent; the norm for other currencies was plus or minus 2.5 per cent. Inside the ERM, the lire has depreciated slowly and steadily against other currencies; the Italians have, in effect, taken full advantage of crawling currency pegs in a loose monetary alliance. Why should they now embrace tight monetary alliance and monetary union? Part of the answer is that the Italians are, strategically, looking backwards and addressing the consequences of the 1992 programme. The Bank of Italy believes that the abolition of exchange controls under the 1992 programme will produce unmanageable exchange rate fluctuations that can only be controlled by monetary unification (*Financial Times*, 18 April 1989). No doubt, the Commission has assiduously encouraged this belief; the connection between 1992 and monetary union is even made symbolically in the Delors plan, where Stage One starts in July 1990, the date when most EC countries are committed to lifting exchange controls. What the Italians and others are not doing is strategically looking forwards and focusing on the consequences of monetary union.

Floating exchange rates over the past decade have been less successful than many economists had hoped; upward appreciation of the yen and deutschmark has not, for example, prevented the build-up of huge surpluses by Germany and Japan. The Delors plan could be represented as a return to a modified Bretton Woods; for 25 years after the Second World War, all the advanced countries lived with fixed exchange rates and realignment of currencies as a last resort. If fixed exhange rates were tolerable then, why should we worry? Our answer would be that we need to worry because, for two sets of reasons, the Delors proposals would have reactionary consequences for most European countries.

1. The working of any fixed exchange rate system depends on the pattern of surpluses and deficits between trade partners. In a simple fixed exchange rate system the burden of adjustment falls on deficit-running countries, which have no choice but to make deflationary adjustments; countries with surpluses are not compelled to make reflationary adjustments. The current proposals for a European system of fixed exchange rates need to be set in the context of the trade and payments imbalances analysed in our first chapter; competitive weakness ensures that all countries except West Germany are in or near payments deficit. A small deterioration in the French or Italian current account would place those countries in the position of deficit runners, like Britain, which in the new order must try to hold their exchange rates by adopting deflationary domestic policies. The pattern of European trade imbalances is such that monetary union is a plan for co-ordinated deflation in a substantial number of European countries.

2. The Delors plan envisages a system for permanent tutelage of national monetary and fiscal policy under the aegis of the new ESCB and the Council of Ministers. This is considerably more reactionary than the old Bretton Woods system, where tutelage was occasionally imposed on individual countries which got into difficulty and required IMF loans, as Britain did in 1976; most countries, most of the time, were free to conduct their own national monetary and fiscal policies. What the Delors plan signifies is the end of national economic management as we have known it in Europe since the end of the Second World War; from Stage Two onwards, all the instruments of national fiscal and monetary policy will be irrelevant or subject to regulation by the ESCB and the Council of Ministers. Does this matter? Not in principle, when it can be represented as simply a necessary step towards European unity. But *how* it will work matters a great deal, and there are very strong indications as to what is intended. This system of permanent tutelage is likely to be operated in an exceedingly restrictive way, because the declared aim is to operate a sound money policy which is beyond political control. In the Delors Report, 'price stability' is the declared objective of monetary policy. And the priority of price stability over the maintenance of employment is to be safeguarded by the constitutional status of the ESCB as an independent institution with no political masters; the Delors Report insists that 'the ESCB

Council should be independent of instructions from national governments and Community authorities'.

In the Delors Report we see a future that means less employment for the weaker and less competitive EC countries. Some EC governments take a more sanguine view because they believe that monetary union will be accompanied by corollary policies which will redress national and regional imbalances and inequalities. The Delors Report speaks of the need for 'greater convergence'. But the discussion of convergence is thoroughly ambiguous. In a discussion of Stage One, Delors mentions the desirability of 'greater convergence of economic performance'. Elsewhere, convergence means convergence of policies to secure the basic objective of union; for example, it is claimed that 'monetary union without a sufficient degree of convergence of economic policies is unlikely to be durable and could be damaging to the Community'. In practice, convergence is likely to mean the enforcement of monetary and fiscal policies which adapt to persistent differences in economic performance and competitiveness. It is hard to see how convergence could mean anything else because the Delors Report only briefly mentions one policy instrument for redressing imbalances. That instrument is EC regional and social policy which, as was argued in Chapter Three, is inadequate and counter-productive.

The 1992 programme instituted largely symbolic liberal market economic changes which satisfied an overriding political motive. The Delors Committee now plans a substantial liberal market economic change which satisfies the same political motive. If the plan is implemented in its present form, it will be a real defeat for all who believe in a liberal collectivist or socialist Europe. But the plan has still to be implemented, and liberal market enthusiasts would do well to remember that the Commission, which has failed the left over social Europe, may not be a sure ally of the right over liberal market Europe. The EC is the sphere of dominance of political motives and calculations which are denied in liberal market economics. Political interests will, for example, ensure the survival of a substantially unreformed CAP which is a massive anomaly for liberal market economics. And political calculations will also limit the application of the principles of free trade; the Commission will defend 'fortress Europe' if that is considered necessary to build European unity. In any case what the Commission does (and fails to do) releases powerful anti-liberal market tendencies and forces;

its broken-backed competition policy condones or even encourages the emergence of a Europe where oligopoly and giant firms abridge the sacred principle of competition.

The Delors Committee's recommendations on monetary union still face many obstacles. The British government will, for reasons quite unconnected with liberal collectivism, attempt to block their acceptance, and other countries may also have misgivings about parts of the scheme. And acceptance in principle is still a long step away from implementation of the details of this particular approach towards greater monetary union in Europe. Even if the restrictive plan for monetary union is implemented, that result may not be decisive and permanent. Reactionary action on monetary union is likely to provoke progressive reaction. In a Europe of unbalanced trade and payments deficits, an attempt to impose deflationary solutions on weaker countries might well provoke sharp reactions. Indeed, it would be surprising if the Commission and Delors had not considered the probability that the consequences of monetary union will be so unpleasant that a more effective social Europe will have to be put into place. Perhaps their calculation is that, as the 1992 programme made monetary union necessary and possible as the next step towards European unity, so monetary union may make social Europe necessary and possible.

It would be unwise, however, to put too much trust in the inevitable progressive logic of history; liberal collectivists and socialists will need to struggle to realise the kind of Europe that they believe in. The need is all the greater since, thus far, the tide has been flowing in the other direction. None the less, it should be possible to secure modifications to the particular banker-dominated, insulated-from-politics form of monetary union at present on offer. And the trend towards more democratic control over legislation and finance by Parliament (possibly, as proposed in Heseltine, 1989, strengthened by a representative second chamber) will be impossible to resist as part of a genuine move towards a united European Community. More democracy does not of course necessarily mean more socialism, but it will provide a forum in which to carry on the struggle. Furthermore, as social Europe is such a confused and inadequate policy response, it will be necessary to make a serious effort to define new policy objectives and instruments of collectivism for Europe in the 1990s.

New directions for socialist policy

On one or two issues it is possible to conceive of broad political alliances where socialists, liberal collectivists and liberal marketeers could work together for change. Reform of the CAP, for example, is a sensible objective on which all could agree, and reform of the CAP can be most effectively pushed by a broad alliance. There is also scope for common action against big business mergers and joint ventures. Nobody, except the businessmen, could be enthusiastic about a Europe where much supra-national merger is unregulated and joint venture is consecrated by the EC; 'restructuring' should not be an all-purpose excuse which allows big business to justify whatever it wants to do. But the issue of merger and joint venture regulation also establishes the limits of political alliance. From a liberal market perspective, merger and joint venture regulation should aim to prevent large firms exploiting consumers. Liberal collectivists and socialists start from the premise that maximising welfare through competition is an irrelevant and unattainable goal; for them, the primary issue is not the exploitation of consumers but the displacement of workers and the redistribution of employment through restructuring. Socialist concern with the (re)location of industry is, of course, anathema to liberal market economists.

From a liberal collectivist and socialist perspective, the overriding priority in the Europe of the 1990s must be producer welfare; the aim should be to increase and redistribute employment so that the low-income and high-unemployment areas of Europe benefit. The danger is that, if monetary union as proposed by Delors goes ahead, EC policy will reinforce the centripetal tendencies which trade creates. The proper role of policy should be to countervail these tendencies. From this point of view, there is no objection to monetary union per se; but the particular form of union proposed by the Delors Committee is objectionable. There is a need to press the case for an expansionary Europe, where EC fiscal and monetary policy privileges employment rather than price stability. If a regime of fixed exchange rates is proposed, there must be policy sanctions which compel reflation by surplus-running countries, especially Germany, instead of tutelage which compels deflation by deficit-running countries. It is, of course, easier to state these general socialist objectives than to secure their adoption in Brussels. To be realistic, the rules of the game proposed in the Delors Report will only be modified if several EC governments establish a 'coalition of the disadvantaged' and press the case for more progressive rules.

Right-wing policians like Mrs Thatcher will in any case wish to block the Delors plan because it infringes 'sovereignty', which to them is a symbolic political issue. In the absence of any significant concession on the rules of the game, the left should also oppose the Delors plan but for rather different, real economic reasons. As long as the instruments of national economic management can be used for progressive purposes, they should not be surrendered unless and until the EC introduces effective supra-national instruments for combatting centripetal tendencies and avoiding deflationary solutions. For the weaker countries, devaluation is the most important of the existing national instruments of management. Devaluation is not a cure, but it is a way of palliating substantial and persistent differences in national manufacturing competitiveness. Or to be more specific, devaluation is a necessary defensive response against the consequences of German industrial supremacy. What the left should do is clearly state the terms on which fixed exchange rates would be acceptable and devaluation might be renounced. The minimum preconditions would be expansionary EC monetary and fiscal policy at a macro level, plus some form of control over the location of industry.

This last condition about micro-economic intervention in location is crucial because there are good reasons for believing that defensive national economic strategies and/or expansionary European macro strategy are inadequate to the problem of the distribution of employment. The logic of national policies on location is a competition for inward investment; in this game of bribery, companies can play off one national government against another, and the weaker regions are at an obvious disadvantage with respect to inducements. New EC regulations are currently curbing the bribery, without putting anything in its place; within the EC free-trade area, there is no incentive for manufacturing companies in successful exporting nations to (re)locate in the poorer regions or countries. As for EC-wide fiscal and monetary expansion, that would increase the overall volume of employment but also reproduce many existing kinds of inequality at higher levels of output and employment. And we do not believe that secondary redistribution is a credible way of palliating these inequalities, even if the social and regional funds are reformed with their expenditure redirected into new objects. No EC country has succeeded in creating a redistributive welfare system that permanently maintains its own unemployed citizens in comfort; it is much less likely that poorer regions or nations with high unemployment rates will be offered a comfortable 'pensioner' status.

The task before us is not to revise socialism in a way that restates the old centrist goal of secondary redistribution; the task is to reinvent socialism in a supra-national context by finding new instruments of positive intervention in the location of industry. This was a task which was effectively abandoned at the national level in the heyday of Keynesianism in the 1950s and 1960s, when it seemed that the minimalist intervention of macro management could solve all problems about the level, composition and distribution of employment; subsequently, national governments simply persisted with expensive and ineffectual regional policies which often bribed firms to do what they would have done anyway. What is required is a centrally organised European policy that influences the locational decisions of private manufacturing firms. In a paper for the British Labour party's policy review, we described how rebates in corporate profits tax could be used to provide substantial inducements for British firms to expand output (Williams et al., 1988). This kind of scheme for value added promotion could be operated at an EC level, so that regions and countries with low incomes or above average unemployment offer profits tax rebates to expanding firms; in central, more advantaged regions, these rebates would be denied. It is not claimed that such a proposal is, in itself, an adequate response to the problem of location, but it does show how, if the issue of location is brought into focus, it is possible to devise new policy instruments. The use of such instruments to influence location policy could ease the payments constraints and counter the regressive distribution of economic activity which was analysed in the first chapter of this book. The biases which have hitherto operated could be reversed, and the integration of the EC could begin to operate in favour of the poor.

In the concluding paragraphs of our last chapter we have, inevitably, turned very briefly to consider solutions. But it was never our aim to produce a political manifesto or a technical report on policy options. In this and the previous chapters we have mainly concentrated on criticising conventional (mis)definitions of Europe's problems and on respecifying these problems so that it is possible to begin to think about how to solve them. Thus, we have attacked orthodox problem definitions on trade and market integration; regional and social policy; and mergers and joint ventures. Throughout, we have tried to make our own political and theoretical *a priori* explicit, while criticising others for presenting politically congenial economic rationalisations. Above all, we have tried to broaden out the debate from the narrow range of issues so far considered in discussion of 1992. We shall be content if we have persuaded our readers of the need to redefine the problems and broaden the issues. That is our immediate contribution to the struggle for Europe.

Bibliography

Ardy, B. (1988), 'The National Incidence of the European Community Budget,' *Journal of Common Market Studies*, Vol. 26, June, pp. 401–29

Avery, G. (1988), 'Agricultural Policy: The Conclusions of the European Council,' *Common Market Law Review*, Vol. 25, No. 3, Autumn, pp. 523–41

Baumol, W. (1965), *Welfare Economics and the Theory of the State*, London, Bell

Caves, R.E. and L. Krause (1980), *Britain's Economic Performance*, Cambridge, Cambridge University Press

Cecchini, P. (1988), *1992 The European Challenge: The Benefits of a Single Market*, Aldershot, Wildwood House

CMLR (1973, 1976 and 1985), *Common Market Law Review*

Cooke, T.E. (1988), *International Mergers and Acquisitions*, Oxford, Blackwell

Cowling, K. (1987), 'Merger Policy, Industrial Strategy and Democracy,' *British Review of Economic Issues*, Vol. 9, No. 21, Autumn, pp. 29–59

Croxford, G., M. Wise and B. Chalkley (1987), 'The Reform of European Regional Fund,' *Journal of Common Market Studies*, Vol. 26, No. 1, September, pp. 25–39

Culbertson, J.M. (1986), 'The Folly of Free Trade,' *Harvard Business Review*, No. 5, September/October, pp. 122–8

Cusumano, M.A. (1985), *The Japanese Automobile Industry*, Cambridge, MA, Harvard University Press

Cutler, T., K. Williams and J. Williams (1986), *Keynes, Beveridge and Beyond*, London, Routledge and Kegan Paul

Daley, A., D. Hitchens and K. Wagner (1985), 'Productivity, Machinery and Skills in a Sample of British and German Manufacturing Plants,' *National Institute Economic Review*, No. 111, February, pp. 48–61

Davis, E. et al. (1989), *1992: Myths and Realities*, London, Centre for Business Strategy, London Business School

Dawson, W., P. Willman, A. Clinton and M. Bamford (1988), *Safety at Work: The Limits of Self-Regulation*, Cambridge, Cambridge University Press

Delors, J. (1987), 'Introduction of the Commission Programme for 1987,' *Bulletin of the EC*, Supplement 1/87, Luxemburg, EC

EC (1985), *White Paper, Completing the Internal Market*, Brussels, European Commission

EC (1985a), *Official Journal of the EC*, December, Brussels

EC (1987), *Regions of the Enlarged Community*, Brussels, European Commission

EC (1987a), *Third Periodic Report on the Social and Economic Situation and Development of the Regions of the Community*, Brussels, European Community

EC (1988), 'The Economics of 1992,' *European Economy*, March

EC (1988a), *European Regional Development Fund, 12th Report*, Brussels, European Commission

EC (1988b), *Eurostats, General Statistics*, Luxemburg, EC

EC (1988c), *Seventeenth Report on Competition Policy*, Brussels, European Commission

EC (1988d), *Research on the Cost of Non-Europe. Basic Findings*, London, HMSO

    Vol. 1, *Executive Summaries*

    Vol. 2, *Studies of the Economics of Integration*

    Vol. 3, *The Completion of the Internal Market: A Survey of European Industry's Perception of Likely Effects*

    Vol. 4, *Border Related Controls and Administrative Formalities*

    Vol. 11, *The EC92 Automobile Sector*

Farrands, C. (1988), 'High Technology Alliances for 1992,' *European Trends*, No. 4, pp. 40–8

Financial Times

Fine, F.L. (1987), 'The Phillip Morris Judgement: Does Article 85 Now Extend to Mergers?' *The European Competition Law Review*, Vol. 8, No. 4, pp. 333–43

Fullerton, B. and A. Gillespie (1988), 'Transport and Communications,' in W. Molle and R. Cappellin (eds), *Regional Impact of Community Policy in Europe*, Aldershot, Gower

Geroski, P.A. (1988), '1992 and European Industrial Structure in the Twenty-first Century,' mimeo, London, London Business School

Goldhar, J. and M. Jelinek (1983), 'Plan for Economies of Scope,' *Harvard Business Review*, November/December, pp. 141–8

Hartley, J. (1987), *Fighting the Recession in Manufacturing*, Bedford, IFS Kempton

Heseltine, M. (1989), *The Challenge of Europe, Can Britain Win?*, London, Weidenfeld and Nicolson

House of Lords Select Committee on Overseas Trade (1985), *Report and Minutes of Evidence*, 'Memorandum submitted by the Department of Trade and Industry,' London, HMSO

House of Lords Select Committee on European Communities (1988), *Agricultural Stabilizers*, London, HMSO

Ingersoll Engineers (1987), *Procurement, Materials Management and Distribution*, Rugby, Ingersoll

Kay, D. (1989), 'Myths and Realities,' in E. Davis et al., *1992: Myths and Realities*, London, London Business School

Keeble, D., J. Offord and S. Walker (1988), *Peripheral Regions in a Community of Twelve Member States*, Luxemburg, Commission of EC

Keeble, D., P. Owens and C. Thompson (1982), *Centrality, Peripherality and EEC Regional Development*, Cambridge, Commission of EC and UK Department of Industry

Kinnock, N. (1988), Speech by Leader of the Labour Party to the Socialist Group of the European Parliament, Glasgow, mimeo

Kinnock, N. (1989), Speech by Leader of the Labour Party at Launch of the British Labour Group of the European Parliament's Campaign on 1992, mimeo

Korah, V. and P. Lasok (1988), 'Phillip Morris and its Aftermath – Merger Control?' *Common Market Law Review*, Vol. 25, No. 2, Summer, pp. 333–68

Leonard, D. (1988), *The Economist Pocket Guide to the European Community*, Oxford, Basil Blackwell/Economist

Lowe, P. (1988), 'The Reform of the Community's Structural Funds,' *The Common Market Law Review*, Vol. 25, No. 3, Autumn, pp. 503–23

Meeks, G. (1977), *Disappointing Marriage: A Case Study of the Gains from Merger*, Cambridge, Cambridge University Press

Molle, W. and R. Cappellin (eds) (1988), *Regional Impact of Community Policy in Europe*, Aldershot, Gower

National Consumer Council (1988), *Consumers and the Common Agricultural Policy*, London, National Consumer Council

Neuberger, H. (1989), *The Economics of 1992*, London, Socialist Group of European Parliament, Labour Group

New Statesman

Nomura Research Institute (1988), *Investment Opportunities in Europe: 1992 from the Point of View of Japanese Companies*, London, Nomura

Padoa-Schioppa, T. (ed.) (1987), *Efficiency, Stability and Equity: A Strategy for the Evolution of the Economic System of the European Community*, Oxford, Oxford University Press

Peat, Marwick and McLintock (1989), *KPMG Deal Watch*, London

Pelkmans, J. and A. Winters (1988), *Europe's Domestic Market*, London, Routledge

Peters, T. and R. Waterman (1982), *In Search of Excellence*, New York, Harper and Row

Porter, M. (1987), 'The State of Strategic Thinking,' *The Economist*, May 23, pp. 21–8

Prais, S.J. (1981), *The Evolution of Giant Firms in Britain*, Cambridge, Cambridge University Press

Pye, R. and G. Lauder (1987), 'Regional Aid for Telecommunications in Europe,' *Telecommunications Policy*, Vol. 11, No. 2, June, pp. 99–113

Roarty, M. (1987), 'The Impact of Common Agricultural Policy,' *National Westminster Bank Review*, February, pp. 12–27

Schonberger, R. (1982), *Japanese Manufacturing Techniques*, New York, Free Press

Steedman, H. and K. Wagner (1987), 'A Second Look at Productivity, Machinery and Skills in Britain and Germany,' *National Institute Economic Review*, Vol. 122, November

Swann, D. (1988), *The Economics of the Common Market*, 6th edn, London, Pelican

Thatcher, M. (1988), *Britain and Europe: Text of the Prime Minister's Speech at Bruges on 20th September 1988*, London, Conservative Political Centre

Touche Ross International (1986), *Completing the Internal Market: A Guide to 1992: An Abridgement of the Cockfield White Paper*, London

Vickers, J. and G. Yarrow (1988), *Privatisation: An Economic Analysis*, Boston, MIT Press

Williams, K. et al. (1983), *Why Are the British Bad at Manufacturing?*, London, Routledge

Williams, K. et al. (1986), 'Accounting for Failure in the Nationalised Industries,' *Economy and Society*, Vol. 15, No. 2, May, pp. 167–219

Williams, K. et al. (1987), 'The End of Mass Production?' *Economy and Society*, Vol. 16, No. 3, August, pp. 405–39

Williams, K. et al. (1988), 'Value Added Promotion,' mimeo, Aberystwyth, Economics Department, University College of Wales

Williams, K. et al. (1989), 'Do Labour Costs Really Matter?' *Work, Employment and Society* (forthcoming)

Williams, K. et al. (1989a), 'Why Take the Stocks Out of Manufacturing?' *International Journal of Production Control* (forthcoming)

Williams, K. et al. (1989b), 'How Far from Japan?' mimeo, Aberystwyth, Economics Department, University College of Wales

About the Authors

The authors are a small team who have published work on manufacturing trade and policy choices.

Their early work examined the conditions and consequences of British manufacturing failure, as well as the nature of the post-war policy settlement which was breaking up in the 1980s.

Differences in national economic performance have always been a major concern. These differences and their consequences are now being analysed explicitly through work on management in different advanced countries and study of the consequences of European integration.

The team's publications include articles and reports as well as a series of books:

K. Williams et al., *Why Are the British Bad at Manufacturing?*, London, Routledge, 1983.

T. Cutler et al., *Keynes, Beveridge and Beyond*, London, Routledge, 1986.

K. Williams et al., *The Breakdown of Austin Rover*, Oxford, Berg, 1987.

K. Williams and J. Williams, *A Beveridge Reader*, London, Allen and Unwin, 1987.

Tony Cutler and Colin Haslam teach in London Polytechnics, at Middlesex and East London, respectively. John and Karel Williams both teach in the Economics Department at University College of Wales, Aberystwyth.

Index